A Bird's-Eye View of THE CITY of BEL

also shewing the exte

Taken from

CW01655325

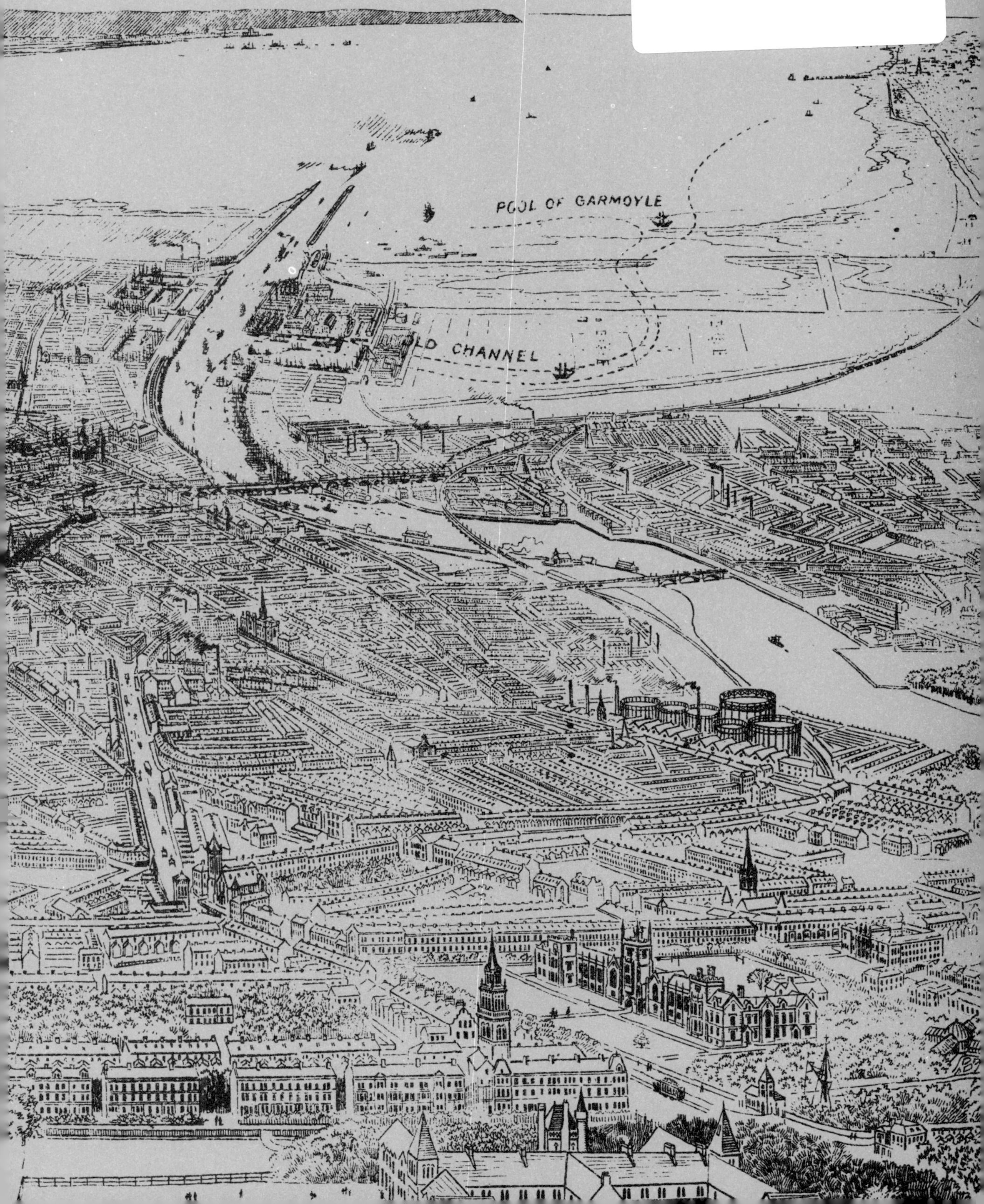

Belfast

The Making of the City

J.C. Beckett *et al.*

First published in hardback in 1983 by
The Appletree Press Ltd
The Old Potato Station
14 Howard Street South
Belfast BT71AP

Tel: + 44 (0) 28 90 243074
Fax: + 44 (0) 28 90 246756
E-mail: reception@appletree.ie
Web-site: www.appletree.ie

This edition published in 2003

© Appletree Press Ltd, 1983, 1988 and 2003

ISBN: 0 86281 8788

All rights reserved. Printed and bound in India. No part of this publication may be reproduced, stored in a retrieval system or transmitted in any form or by any means, electronic, mechanical, photocopying, recording or otherwise, without the prior permission of the copyright holder.

Published in hardback by Appletree Press
for Lagan Books.

ISBN: 0 86281 877 X

Thanks to the Ulster Museum, Belfast and the Linenhall Library, Belfast for their assistance in the illustration of this book.

Cover photographs: Welch Collection, Ulster Museum and Hogg Collection, Ulster Museum. Photographs reproduced with the kind permission of the Trustees of the National Museums & Galleries of Northern Ireland.

Front endpaper illustration: A Bird's-Eye View of the City of Belfast by D. Hanna, 1883.
Back endpaper: Plan of the town of Belfast by J. Thompson 1822 (George Benn, *History of the town of Belfast*, Belfast, 1823).

Contents

Preface

That river-straddling, hill-rimmed town (John Hewitt)
Belfast devout and profane and hard (Louis MacNeice)

For a city which is famed far and wide for its linen and its iron ships rather than for its contribution to art or literature, Belfast has produced a surprising number of artists, poets and writers whose names are well-known; and many books have been published on its geography, its history and on many special aspects of its life since George Benn's pioneer *History of the town of Belfast* (1823). Not all the authors have been Ulstermen: indeed the present writer notes with pride that both David Owen, who wrote *A Short History of the Port of Belfast* (1917) and a *History of Belfast* (1921) and Emrys Jones, *A Social Geography of Belfast* (1966) were Welshmen. Many other books on Belfast and Northern Ireland have consisted of articles by several authors combined in a single volume. The first, I believe, was the *Guide to Belfast and the Adjacent Counties* published in 1874 to mark the occasion of the first meeting in the city of the British Association for the Advancement of Science. The scientists had been holding their annual gatherings at various centres in the British Isles since 1821, but Belfast was the first to offer the visitors a Guide or comprehensive regional survey covering the city and its neighbourhood. The Queen's University of Belfast, which was to become the main centre of scientific research in Ulster, was not established until 1849 and the Guide was written by members of the Belfast Naturalists Field Club, who prepared another Guide for the 1902 meeting. I believe the example set by Belfast has been followed ever since by the different centres which have hosted the British scientists in rotation. The last Belfast meeting was held in 1952, when a comprehensive work on Belfast in its regional setting was edited by Emrys Jones.

The Field Club, founded in 1863 for the practical study of natural science and archaeology, had been preceded by the Belfast Natural History and Philosophical Society. In a society in which the division between protestants and Roman Catholics dominated life many intelligent citizens found a common interest in 'natural history' in the widest sense, and while these clubs remained predominantly protestant and in protestant control, even if many of their leaders would have called themselves protestant agnostics, they always contained catholics. Indeed it is suggested in one of the essays which follows that they became popular precisely because they were neutral in outlook.

More recently the BBC has sponsored three multi-authored books in the general field of local history; two paperbacks entitled *Ulster Since 1800* edited by T. W. Moody and J. C. Beckett and subtitled political and economic (1954) and social (1957) and the hardback *Belfast, the origin and growth of an industrial city,* (1967) edited by J. C. Beckett and R. E. Glasscock. The present volume thus perpetuates an honourable tradition in Belfast publishing. One advantage of having several authors is that a diversity of subjects can be handled with authority by chosen experts even if, in theory, the overall view of a single author gives a book more character and unity.

The present authors are all very familiar with their given topics and they are so diversified that it is not easy to think of serious omissions. I am delighted and honoured to have been invited to preface this volume.

E. Estyn Evans

Foreword

Every generation looks again at its past, sometimes with new evidence, always with new perspectives. This book takes as its theme the history of Belfast in the nineteenth century and the Edwardian era—its politics and intellectual life, industry and commerce, artists and writers. It tries to convey through word and photograph something of the city and of its atmosphere so that we can more easily imagine and understand the impact of this remarkable century.

History is apt to highlight the achievers, the 'big men' of any society, and in this respect this book may differ little from previous histories of Belfast. Quite rightly it honours the politicians, churchmen, industrialists, scientists and artists who made notable contributions to the life of the city. The Donegalls, Cooke, Harland, Kelvin, Pirrie and others all figure in these pages just as they do in the street names; any history of Belfast would be incomplete without them. But what of the unnamed thousands who lived in the small Victorian streets and whose labour produced the linen, the rope and the ships for which Belfast was known the world over by the end of the century? What of those who lived in Flax, Hemp and Mill streets, in Chemical and Utility, in Eia, Electric and Eliza? And those for whom the wider world was only a name on a wall—Delhi and Damascus, Trafalgar and Waterloo, Nubia and the Yukon? They have no monuments; they have left their names, if at all, in rent books, wage lists and census returns. They can be discovered and brought to life only through memories, and the archives of the Public Record Office, Ulster Museum and the like, or, as in this book, through the eyes of early photographers who had the foresight to record everyday scenes of people at work and, less often, at play.

Although streets may not be named after the 'unknowns' they were built *for* them and it is these same people who lie behind the most outstanding feature of Belfast's nineteenth-century history, namely its phenomenal population growth. As we are reminded by the many contributors to this book the population grew from about 20,000 or so in 1801 to almost 350,000 a century later, an increase that would tax the ingenuity and resources of any city in this century, let alone in the last. When large numbers of people live together systems have to be devised to govern behaviour, to allocate space, to provide employment, shelter, food and water. Belfast did its best to grapple with these problems; it was no worse than most Victorian cities and better than some. Nevertheless we look back on good and bad results. On the one hand we see the founding of schools and what was later to become a university, the erection of civic buildings, new churches, libraries and theatres, and the setting aside of space for public recreation and enjoyment: on the other, we see dreadful overcrowding, exploitation, appalling working conditions, chronic illness and outbreaks of class and sectarian strife. Whatever the achievements of nineteenth-century Belfast—and there were many in the industrial and cultural fields—a high price was paid in the quality of life of the majority of its people.

Belfast citizens of the early nineteenth century were even nearer to the countryside than they are today when visitors envy them their daily views of the Cave Hill and of the green slopes of Co. Down. In 1800 Belfast was a modest town clustered around the Farset and the shallows of the Lagan estuary. When the Donegall family, who virtually owned the town, built their new house at Ormeau in 1807 they moved into the country. They could hardly have foreseen that within a century their country estate would be swallowed up by the town as it expanded, not only through the arrival of more and more people, but by the frequent boundary changes that were necessary to incorporate them within the city. The Donegalls were certainly aware of the rapid growth but they were to play little part in the transformation of the small eighteenth-century town into the great industrial city of a century later, except, as Dr Maguire reminds us 'by disappearing from the scene at the right time'. Their land was sold or rented on long leases; new men, industrialists and entrepreneurs, acquired land and took opportunities to turn Ulster's raw materials, especially flax, into finished products. The growth of industry took strange twists and turns. Who could foresee that the introduction of cotton spinning in the Poor House would turn out to be a major influence on industrialization? Or again, that a new linen industry would rise from the ashes of Mulholland's cotton mill which burned to the ground, disastrously so it seemed, in 1828?

To the new industries and to the relative wealth that they generated in other trades came many thousands of people, not only from nearby Antrim and Down but from the depths of the Ulster countryside and beyond; poverty and periodic famine drove them towards the regular wages and apparent security of the town. It was these thousands who made Belfast a city and who gave it its present character, its accent and its history. While one is nearer to the spirit of the community in Smithfield or at a bus-stop in Bradbury Place than one can ever be in the pages of a book, the use of photographs gives us some feel for the Belfast of a century ago.

When I lived in the city and worked at Queen's I formed the impression that there were more 'historians' in Ulster than in any other part of the British Isles! A deep and abiding interest in the past has been nurtured over the years by many institutions and societies, notable among them Queen's University, the Ulster Museum, the Ulster Archaeological Society and, more recently, the Folk Museum and the Ulster Architectural Heritage Society. Individuals have also played prominent parts, none more so than those doyens of Ulster's history and geography professors J. C. Beckett and E. Estyn Evans, both of whom happily continue a long-standing tradition by contributing in different ways to this book. All these represent the good side of history—the search for a deeper understanding and insight into the evolution of a society. Unfortunately history also has its bad side. It saddens me to write this on a day when a student has been found dead in the University area, yet another victim of the turbulent political and social history of the city or of what John Hewitt describes as 'our idiosyncratic tensions and eruptions'. This inhumanity remains a blot on a city with a history which is distinguished in so many other ways. If this book, which will be of interest to all Belfast people, can contribute in any small way to mutual tolerance of opposing attitudes and aspirations, then it will take its own place in the history of the city which it seeks to describe. That is my best wish for its success.

Robin E. Glasscock
St John's College, Cambridge

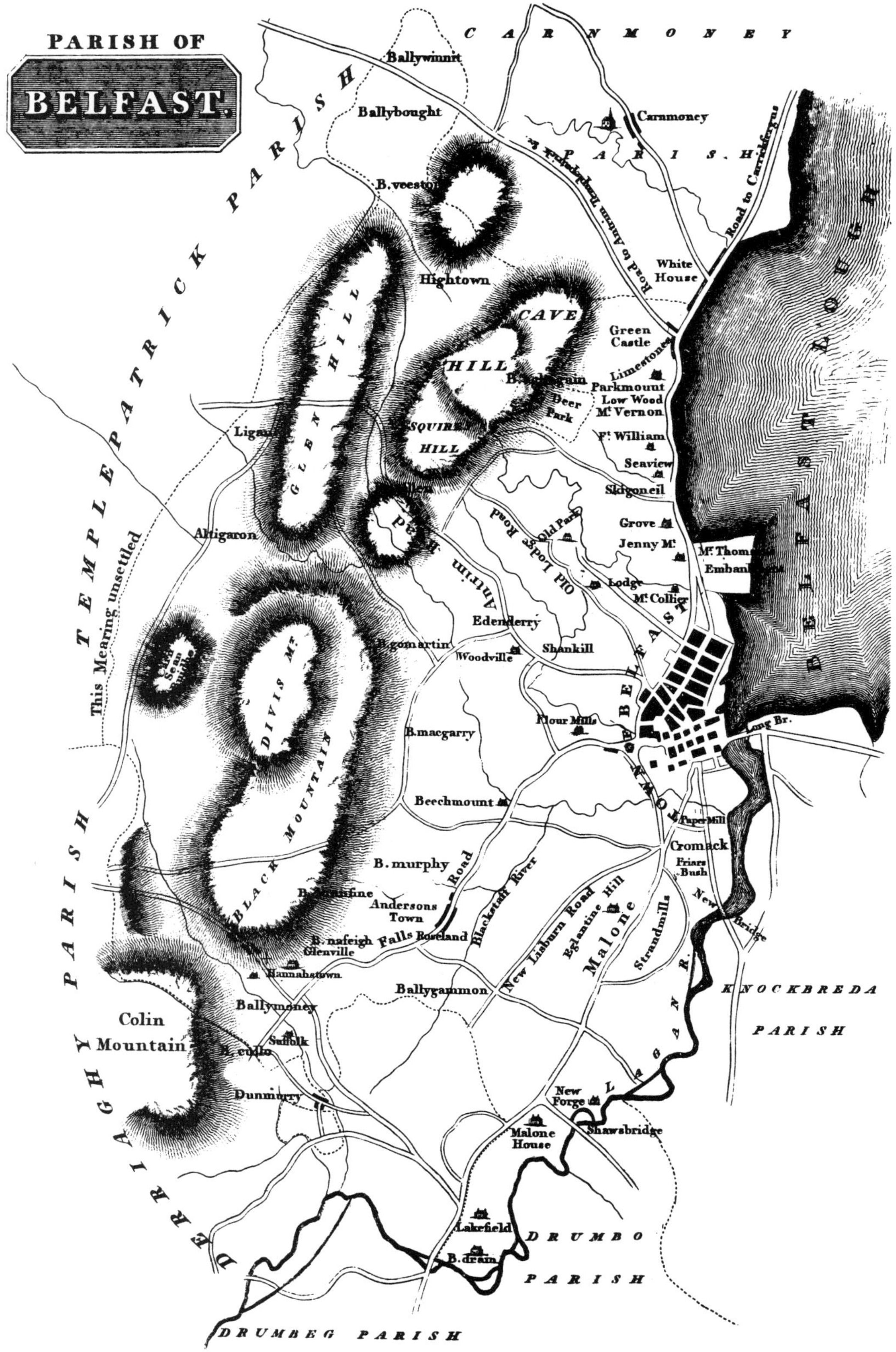

(from Benn, George, *History of the Town of Belfast,* Belfast, 1823)

1. Belfast to the end of the eighteenth century

J. C. Beckett

The history of Belfast as a town begins in the early seventeenth century. But the name is much older than this; and whereas the town was English in origin the name is Gaelic. There is some disagreement about its precise meaning; but it certainly contains reference to a sandbank, situated not far from where the Queen's Bridge now stands; and this sandbank enabled travellers to ford the Lagan at low tide. Such a crossing-place was important both in peace and in war, and was therefore worth defending. It was for this reason that the Normans, who invaded eastern Ulster in the late twelfth century, built a castle at Belfast. No trace of this remains; but it probably stood on or near the same site as the later castle, which is still commemorated in street names: Castle Lane and Castle Place.

Norman power receded in the fourteenth century; and eastern Ulster, including Belfast, came once more under the rule of Gaelic chieftains. But in the reign of Queen Elizabeth an attempt was made to establish an English settlement in the area; and it is now that we hear, for the first time, of a proposal to build a town at Belfast. This came to nothing, however; and it was not until the reign of James I that a new and more successful effort was made. Since James was king of Scotland as well as of England both Scottish and English settlers were involved. But it was to an Englishman, Sir Arthur Chichester (later Lord Chichester of Belfast) that James granted the castle of Belfast and a large area round it. It was under Chichester's direction that the planning and building of the town were undertaken; and for the next two centuries the Chichester family was to exercise a powerful influence on the life of Belfast.

In 1613, when Belfast was still in a very early stage of development, it received from James I a charter erecting it into a corporate borough. The king's motive was political. He was about to call a parliament in Ireland; he wanted to make sure of a protestant majority in the house of commons; and to that end he created many new boroughs, each entitled to return two members. It must be admitted, however, that many of these new boroughs, though very small at the time, were chosen with an eye to their future development, and several of them became substantial towns. But no one could have forseen, in 1603, that Belfast would far outstrip them all.

Sir Arthur Chichester, from a 17th century engraving.

The system of government laid down in the charter was very narrowly based. The town was to be administered by a sovereign (or, as we should say, mayor) and twelve burgesses; and the first holders of these offices were nominated in the charter. The burgesses were to hold office for life and vacancies were to be filled by the sovereign and the remaining burgesses. The sovereign was to hold office for one year and was to be elected by the burgesses. There was also a class of 'freemen' or 'free commoners'; but they had little share in the government of the town and none at all in the choice of the town's two MPs, who were to be elected by the sovereign and burgesses. In practice, the government of the town was even more narrowly restricted than these terms would indicate. The charter gave considerable power to Chichester and his successors as Lords of the Castle; and the fact that they owned the whole of the land on which the town was built made their authority almost irresistible. In practice, it was they who nominated not only the sovereign but also the two members of parliament by whom the interests of the town were nominally represented. For a long time this state of affairs was accepted with little or no complaint; but in the more liberal atmosphere of the eighteenth century it was to become a source of grievance.

The economic life of the new town depended on commerce rather than on manufactures. There was some brick-making, but only to supply local needs; and attempts to establish iron-works had little success. It was as a market for the surrounding countryside and as a port that Belfast grew steadily, if not very quickly, in importance. This growth was assisted by the continuing influx of English and Scottish settlers into south Antrim and north Down. It was through Belfast that they exported their surplus produce and imported what they needed from elsewhere. For centuries before this Carrickfergus

Sir Arthur Chichester presenting the charter of Belfast to the sovereign and burgesses in Cornmarket, by John Carey, 1884 (from R. M. Young *Historical Notices of Old Belfast and its Vicinity,* Belfast, 1896).

had been the principal port in the area; and what is now 'Belfast Lough' was then 'Carrickfergus Lough'. But by the 1680s the seaborne trade of Belfast was worth five or six times that of Carrickfergus and it continued to increase. In the seventeenth century this trade was, for the most part, a coasting or cross-channel trade; but there was some direct trade with the continent also. Later, this was to increase considerably, and a trade with North America was to develop.

The growth of Belfast was encouraged by the fact that it suffered little from the widespread warfare that dislocated economic life over most of Ireland in the 1640s and 1650s. Indeed, it may even have benefited. The large number of Scottish and English troops sent to Ulster had to be fed and clothed and kept supplied with military stores; and the amount of business thus created was of advantage to the merchants of Belfast. It was, for example, at this period that George Macartney, who later came to dominate the commercial life of the town, laid the foundation of his fortunes.

This period was significant in another way also. To begin with, the population of Belfast had been mainly of English extraction and attached to the established church, the Church of Ireland. Now, there was a considerable influx of Scottish presbyterians, and Belfast began to acquire the presbyterian character that marked it so strongly in the eighteenth century, and later. The presbyterians, though they had taken arms against the ecclesiastical policy of Charles I, were attached to the principle of monarchy; and they were horrified at the king's execution. At a meeting in Belfast, on 15 February 1649, they condemned it as 'an act so horrible as no history, divine or human, ever had a precedent to the like'. Naturally enough,

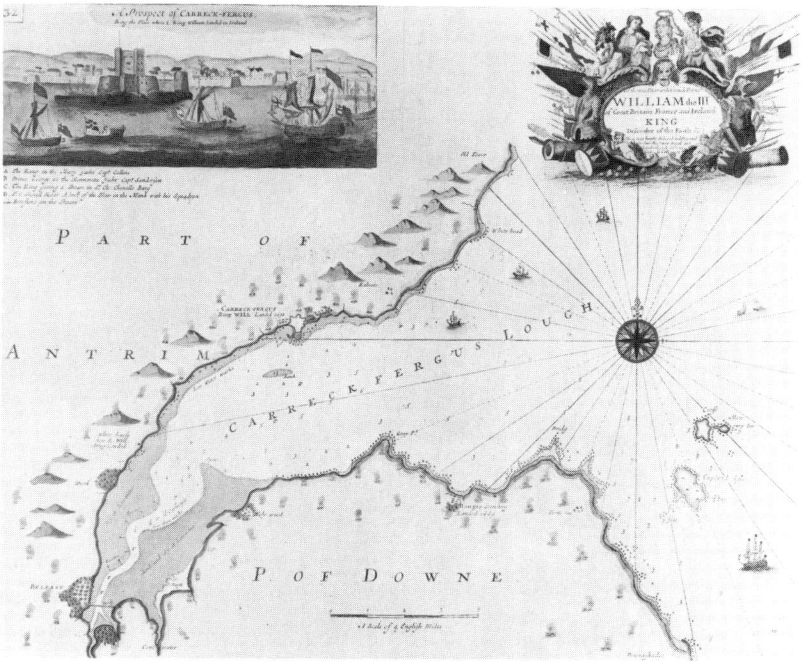

Chart of 'Carrickfergus Lough' (*Great Britain's Coasting Pilot,* Captain Greenvile, c. 1693).

then, Belfast welcomed the restoration of Charles II a little more than eleven years later.

The Restoration did not bring the presbyterians the security they had expected; but for Belfast it marked the opening of a period during which its economic growth was to continue even more rapidly than before. Already, not quite fifty years after the grant of the charter, it was well on the way to becoming one of the principal ports in Ireland. Yet it was still, even by seventeenth-century standards, a small place. In area, it can hardly have exceeded a quarter of a square mile; and much of this space was open ground. The only building of any distinction was the castle; there was no town hall; the parish church had barely recovered from its use for military purposes during the interregnum. The total population was probably not less than a thousand, but can hardly have been much more.

The size of the town was, however, less significant than the resources of the hinterland that it served. Eastern Ulster, recovering rapidly from the long period of warfare and political unrest, produced a large surplus of exportable goods and provided a market for imports from Great Britain and the continent; and a large proportion of this trade passed through Belfast. Beef, butter, hides, tallow and corn were shipped to England and Scotland and to various parts of Europe, expecially to France. Trade with North America, which was later to expand greatly, was still on a relatively small scale. In return, came coal, cloth, wine, brandy, paper, timber, tobacco. Much of this trade was carried in English or Scottish ships;

but the number of Belfast-owned ships was increasing: there were twenty-nine, at least, in the early 1660s; twenty years later they had risen to sixty-seven. Few of these ships, and none of more than fifty tons burthen, had been built at Belfast; but the number, though small, indicates that the town already had the beginnings, at least, of a ship-building industry.

Among the merchants who profited by this growing prosperity the most important was George Macartney; and he was also one of the few who initiated any major enterprise for the good of the town in general. It was at his suggestion, and under his supervision, that water was brought in wooden pipes from a mill-dam just beyond the western boundary of the town and made available to the inhabitants 'at three several conduits running in the streets'. Before this, it would seem, they had depended for their water-supply on the river Farset (not yet covered in) which ran down High Street and was, as they complained, 'very much defiled'.

The peaceful period that followed the Restoration came to an end in 1689. In March of that year the Jacobite army scattered the protestant forces at Dromore; and when the news reached Belfast some of the inhabitants fled in terror to Scotland. But the situation soon changed. In August, Schomberg arrived with a Williamite army of 10,000 men; and thereafter Belfast was safely remote from the scene of conflict. There is nothing to suggest that the warfare of this period did anything to retard the growth of the town. A return of the duties collected at Irish ports in 1697—8 shows Belfast in fourth place, exceeded only by Dublin, Cork and Waterford.

It is worth noting that in this year exports from Belfast to England

Representation of the burning of Belfast Castle in 1708, by J & J. Carey, 1895 (Ulster Museum).

included linen cloth to the value of over £6,000. Earlier, the export trade of Belfast had depended almost wholly on agricultural products, expecially beef, butter, hides and tallow; but by the 1690s the linen industry was becoming firmly established in Ireland, and especially in the north. Nevertheless, for a long time the bulk of the export trade passed through Dublin, where the credit facilities required by the merchants were more readily available. Gradually, however, Belfast's share of the trade increased: by the 1770s more than a fifth of all the linen exported from Ireland was shipped from Belfast, and the proportion was rising. In the next decade the erection of the White Linen Hall (on the site now occupied by the City Hall) was a striking indication of the importance that the town attached to the linen trade.

Though eighteenth-century Belfast benefited greatly from the linen industry, the town itself was still at this period a centre of commerce, not of manufacture. This predominance of commercial, rather than industrial, activity had two important consequences. In the first place, the growth of population was gradual.During the latter half of the eighteenth century it rose from around 8,000 to around 20,000. During the first half of the nineteenth century, with manufacturing industry firmly established, it rose from 20,000 to 100,000. In the second place, the leading citizens of eighteenth-century Belfast were not captains of industry but professional men and merchants; and the evidence would suggest that the influence of those who were interested in learning and literature was more pervasive than it was to be in the much larger and wealthier city of the next century.

The cultural life of eighteenth-century Belfast was strongly influenced by the close links that Ulster presbyterians still maintained with Scotland. There was a steady flow of young men to the Scottish universities, and especially to Edinburgh and Glasgow, from which they returned to become ministers, or to practise medicine, or, though less often, to engage in commerce. It was largely through them that Belfast was kept in touch with the stimulating development of philosophical and political ideas characteristic of Scotland at this period. The liberal outlook for which the town was noted in the later decades of the eighteenth century was due, mainly if not wholly, to this Scottish influence.

The presence of a substantial number of educated people no doubt helps to account for the fact that Belfast already had an established printing-press by the 1690s, at a time when there was hardly a printer in England north of the Trent. The initiative was taken by William Crawford, a well-to-do merchant. In 1694, when he was sovereign of the town, he induced Patrick Neill, a Glasgow printer, to settle in Belfast; and Neill brought with him his brother-in-law, James Blow, who took over the business on Neill's death, some ten years later. Blow himself survived until 1759 and he is by

The Exchange and Assembly Rooms, from an engraving by Thomas Malton, 1793 (Ulster Museum).

far the best known of early Belfast printers.

It is characteristic of the period, and of the place, that a high proportion of what was printed consisted of sermons and pamphlets, often controversial, by presbyterian ministers, and of Bibles, psalm-books and presbyterian catechisms. But Blow did not cater only for presbyterians. In 1722 he printed the church catechism in Irish, 'with the English placed over against it in the same *karakter*'. And he did not confine himself to theology and theological controversy; for in 1722 he published an edition of the works of the sixteenth-century Scottish poet and satirist, Sir David Lindsay. At this time Blow was probably the only printer in Belfast; but before very long others established themselves. It was one of these, Francis Joy, who in 1737 gave the town its first regular newspaper, the *Belfast News-Letter*.

The publication of books, of pamphlets and of a newspaper would suggest a fairly high degree of literacy among the population in general; but we know little about the early history of schools in Belfast. The corporation appointed a schoolmaster in 1648; and the Commonwealth government took over responsibility for his salary in 1655. But there is nothing to indicate where he conducted his school. In the 1660s the earl of Donegall, nephew and successor of the first Lord Chichester, built and endowed a new school-house adjoining the parish church. This was a 'Latin school' of the traditional kind; and, as time went on, there was an increasing number of parents who wanted a simpler and more immediately useful form of education for their sons. To meet this need private schools were established, in which reading, writing and arithmetic were the basic subjects. The most famous of these private schoolmasters was David Manson, who undertook to teach his pupils 'to spell, read, and understand the English tongue without the discipline of the rod'. He proved so successful that he had to move to larger premises, first in High Street and then in Donegall Street, where he had a house specially built to accommodate boarders.

Manson's school, though popular, provided only a fairly elementary type of education. The Latin school maintained by the Donegall family seems to have declined greatly in the latter half of the eighteenth century; and, in any case, it was too closely associated with the established church to be acceptable to the presbyterians. But they were much concerned about higher education, and especially about the education of candidates for the ministry. From time to time, since the 1690s, they had considered the possibility of establishing in some Ulster town an institution that would provide ministerial training, so that they should no longer be completely

High Street, from a drawing by John Nixon, 1786 (Ulster Museum).

dependent upon the Scottish universities. By the later eighteenth century it was obvious that Belfast had the best claim to be the seat of any such institution; and it was natural, therefore, that presbyterians should take a leading part in the founding of the Belfast Academy in 1785. But the Academy, though successful as a school, did not provide, as they had hoped it would, courses of a university character; and it was not until after the establishment of the Academical Institution, in 1810, that Ulster presbyterian ministers could receive their training at home.

The founding of the Academy was an indication of the growth in numbers and prosperity of the professional and commercial classes for whose sons the new school was intended to cater. But there was, and had long been, a great deal of poverty in the town. A fund for the relief of the poor had been established in the early seventeenth century; but it depended upon occasional gifts and bequests and was quite inadequate to maintain any regular system of relief. Since the corporation was unable, or unwilling, to take any effective action, a voluntary society, the Belfast Charitable Society, was established in 1752 to deal with the problem. Its plan was to build a poorhouse, with a hospital or infirmary attached, and to establish a school for poor children. The raising of the necessary funds took much longer than had been expected; and it was not until 1771 that the foundation stone of the building, which is still in use, was laid; and it was not until 1774 that it was ready for occupation. John Wesley, who visited the Poor House in 1778, was very favourably impressed; but a few years later John Howard, who viewed it with the eyes of an expert, was less well satisfied.

The building of the Poor House and the foundation of the Academy showed that the people of Belfast, though virtually

The Poor House, (from *Twenty-one Views of Belfast and its Neighbourhood,* Dublin, 1836).

excluded by the terms of the charter from any effective share in the government of the town, were prepared to take action on their own initiative. They were prepared, also, to express their views on public affairs, the more readily, perhaps, because they had no voice in choosing the town's representatives in parliament. In 1775 'a general meeting of the principal inhabitants', with the sovereign in the chair, approved an address to the king, deploring 'the horror of civil war' in America and urging the king to make peace with the colonists. There was an element of self-interest in this, for Belfast had a very valuable trade with North America. But there was also a good deal of sympathy with the colonists. This arose partly from the fact that during the preceding sixty years there had been an almost continuous stream of emigration from Ulster to North America, so that many of the colonists were of Ulster birth or parentage. Besides this, there was a growing conviction that Irishmen, like the Americans, had good reason to complain of the way in which they were treated by the government in London. The events of the next few years were to enable those who shared this conviction to organize support for their views and to secure at least a partial redress of their grievances.

The army in Ireland had been so weakened by the withdrawal of men for service in America that it was no longer adequate for the defence of the country; and when France joined the Americans early in 1778 the danger of invasion seemed real. It was to meet this danger that Volunteer companies, quite independent of government control, were established in every part of Ireland. In this movement for self-defence Belfast can claim to have taken the lead. In April 1778 the American privateer, Paul Jones, after making successful raids on the coasts of Cumberland and Scotland, sailed into Belfast Lough, where he engaged and captured a king's ship. In response to this threat the people of Belfast quickly raised two companies of Volunteers; and this example was soon followed elsewhere. There was no invasion; the Volunteers were not called upon to fight; instead, they took to politics, and it was with their help that Henry Grattan was able to establish the legislative independence of the Irish parliament.

In Belfast, as elsewhere, the Volunteers were drawn from the middle and upper ranks of society: each man was expected to provide his own uniform and his own weapons, and to have sufficient command of his time to attend regular drills. The Volunteers were also a protestant body; for at this period it was still illegal for a Roman Catholic to carry arms. In Belfast this restiction can have had little practical effect on the composition of the Volunteer companies; for the Roman Catholic population, though growing, was still small; and it consisted mainly of workmen and their families. By 1784, however, they were numerous enough to provide themselves with a church—St Mary's, in what is now Chapel

Belfast from Cromac Wood, by Jonathan Fisher, 1772 (Ulster Museum).

Lane; and on 30 May of that year the Volunteers paraded in full dress and attended Mass, along with a large number of other protestant inhabitants. But the Volunteers, though anxious to show good will toward their Roman Catholic neighbours, and though advocating the easing, or total removal, of the disabilities under which they still laboured, undoubtedly shared Henry Grattan's conviction that the government of Ireland would nevertheless remain in protestant hands.

The political activity aroused by the Volunteer movement did not soon die away. Having secured the legislative independence of the Irish parliament the Volunteers next demanded a reform of the electoral system; and this was a demand likely to attract support in Belfast. A public meeting of the inhabitants, held in January 1784, approved a petition to the house of commons in which it was pointed out that the two members returned by Belfast were the nominees of Lord Donegall and could not be regarded as in any sense the representatives of the population of the town. But though the terms of this petition were unanimously approved at the meeting, a division between the more cautious and the more ardent advocates of reform had already appeared. The latter thought that the attitude of the *Belfast News-Letter,* the town's only newspaper, was not sufficiently determined; and to provide a mouthpiece for their own views they established, in 1783, another newspaper, the *Mercury.* The *Mercury* did not, however, survive very long; and its disappearance in 1786 marks a temporary decline in the influence of the more extreme reformers. The outbreak of the French Revolution, a few years later, was to revive and extend their activity. In 1792 they once again established a paper of their own, the *Northern Star.* It survived for only five years; but during that brief period it acquired an enduring reputation by its high literary quality.

In Belfast, as in so many other places, the early stages of the French Revolution were regarded with approval; and the fall of the

Wolfe Tone, from R. R. Madden's *The United Irishmen, their Lives and Times* (Ulster Museum).

Bastille was enthusiastically welcomed. But as the revolutionary leaders became more extreme in their demands and more violent in their methods a division of opinion appeared. There were many who now saw the revolution as a threat to all authority, religious as well as civil; while others regarded events in France as providing a model which Ireland should follow. Among the latter were many who had been active in the Volunteer movement and who still resented their failure to secure the reforms they had demanded. Now, encouraged by French example, they prepared to renew the struggle. It was to this end that they founded, in 1791, the Society of United Irishmen, which had as its object the establishment of a democratic parliamentary system under which all citizens would have equal rights, irrespective of their religious denomination. Though the Society had its origin in Belfast, its headquarters was established in Dublin; and its later activities belong to national rather than to local history. Some remnant of the radical tradition that the Society represented survived in the Belfast of the early nineteenth century. But its driving force had gone; and within little more than a generation it had virtually disappeared.

Though the political events of the later eighteenth century occupied so much space in the newspapers of the time, and though the daily routine of the ordinary citizen was sometimes interrupted by popular disturbance or by military activity, the regular business of everyday life went on and the economic development of Belfast continued unchecked. The late 1770s saw the introduction of cotton-spinning by power-driven machinery; and this later proved to be the first step towards turning Belfast into an industrial city. In 1783 a Chamber of Commerce was established. In the following year the foundation stone of the White Linen Hall was laid. In 1785 a new body, commonly called the Ballast Board, was appointed to take charge of the harbour, where it made great improvements. To the average Belfast businessman these developments, which helped to expand the trade of the town, may well have seemed of more immediate importance than the course of politics, at home or abroad. This was certainly the impression left on a French visitor who passed through the town in 1797 and reported that he found the people much more ready to complain about the price of sugar or linen than to take any interest in the course of the war then raging in Europe.

The Green Linen Market and commercial buildings, Donegall Street, Belfast, by T. M. Baynes (*Ireland Illustrated,* 1831).

It would, however, be a mistake to put much weight on a superficial judgement of this kind. The interest in political questions was genuine, even though it might only rarely be allowed to supersede the routine duties of everyday life. And the people of Belfast had other interests also. The import of books and the presence of book-sellers shows that there was a sizeable reading public; and it was to serve this public that the Belfast Reading Society was founded in the 1780s. In 1792 it broadened its aims and changed its name to the Belfast Society for Promoting Knowledge; and when, later on, it was provided with accommodation in the White Linen Hall it acquired the name by which it is now best known, the Linen Hall Library.

The early establishment of a printing press shows that Belfast, even in the 1690s, had writers as well as readers. But it was mainly pamphlets, ecclesiastical or political, sermons and other religious works that gave employment to the printers. There was little creative writing in prose or verse; and none of it, apart from a few poems by William Drennan, has stood the test of time. It is worth noting that in a century when the theatre was regarded as a natural starting-point for the aspiring author only two plays by Belfast writers are known to have reached the stage. Neither had much success, even in Belfast, and neither was acted anywhere else.

This absence of playwrights did not result from lack of opportunity, for the theatre was very popular in eighteenth-century Belfast, despite the suspicion with which it was traditionally viewed by presbyterians. The town's first theatre was opened in the 1730s; and at that time it was the only Irish theatre outside Dublin and Cork, though other towns soon followed. These provincial theatres depended mainly on touring companies; and the plays performed were, with few exceptions, plays that had been successful in London: the development of a distinctive Irish school of drama was still in the distant future. Nevertheless, a local flavour could be given to a performance by having a specially written prologue recited by one of the cast. Such a prologue was written by a young Ulster lawyer, Hugh George Macklin, and recited in the Belfast theatre on 25 February 1793. One passage in it reflects very clearly the pride that Belfast people of the period took in their town:

> And have not here our souls with Freedom glow'd;
> Has she not here long fix'd her lov'd abode?
> Yes—and old time shall yet, with glad surprize,
> View in Belfast a second Athens rise.

And if there was, indeed, any period at which Belfast could claim to be, as some of the inhabitants liked to think, 'the Athens of the North', it was during the closing decades of the eighteenth century.

2. Lords and landlords —the Donegall Family

W. A. Maguire

When George Augustus, second marquis of Donegall, astonished his tenants by coming to live among them early in 1802 he was the first of the Chichesters to do so for nearly a hundred years. Ever since the old Castle near the High Street had burned down in 1708 they had lived in England. He himself, born in London in 1769, had been brought up either there, in the family's town residence in fashionable St James's Square, or in the great house his father had built at Fisherwick in Staffordshire (hence some of Belfast's street names). Since succeeding to this father's titles and estates in 1799 Lord Donegall had continued to live in England, spending money as fast as he could borrow it, until even his very large income of £30,000 a year (a couple of million in modern money) was so encumbered by debt that he was unable to get any more credit. This was why he was persuaded to retire with his family to Belfast, where it would be cheaper to live and easier for him to dodge his numerous creditors. His exile to Belfast was intended to be only temporary. As it turned out, he was to live there for the rest of his life.

With him came his wife Anna and their children (there were to be seven in all, all sons) and his wife's relations, the Mays. The story of

Belfast from Ormeau in 1805, after the drawing by T. C. Thompson (Ulster Museum).

the Donegalls often sounds like the plot of a sensational novel of the period, and Lady Donegall's life was particularly dramatic. Anna May was the illegitimate daughter of a man named Edward May from Waterford who, though he came of a respectable family, and later inherited his father's baronetcy, lived a life that was anything but respectable. He is said to have run off with the wife of a Liverpool merchant, before going to London where he ran a gaming house and became a shady moneylender. In 1795, when the young Lord Belfast (as the heir to the Donegall title was called) was in the debtors' prison in London, May got him released and persuaded him to marry Anna. Thereafter the Mays stuck closely to Lady Belfast and her weak-willed husband, and when Belfast became Donegall their fortunes were made. For the rest of their lives the elder Mays lived with the Donegalls, and were even buried in the Chichester vault at Carrickfergus. Edward May junior became his brother-in-law's chief agent, and was appointed both sovereign (mayor) and vicar of Belfast through Donegall's influence. His brother Stephen followed their father as MP for Belfast, later got the lucrative post of collector of customs, and was also sovereign for many years. By acquiring long leases of parts of the Donegall property at low rents they built up a considerable estate, commemorated in such names as May Street and Maysfield.

For the first few years the Donegalls lived in a house on the corner of Donegall Place (known then as Linen Hall Street) and Donegall

The Royal Hotel (formerly Donegall House), Donegall Place, photographed in the 1870s (Ulster Museum).

Square, opposite the site of Robinson & Cleaver's store. At that time Donegall Square, with the White Linen Hall at its centre where the City Hall now stands, was the very edge of the town. The fine new houses of the area were all inhabited by leading citizens and had not yet begun to be turned into commercial premises (Donegall House itself was to suffer this fate in 1824, when it became the Royal Hotel). In 1807, however, while keeping Donegall House as a town residence, the Donegalls moved into the country, to Ormeau, a considerable distance from Belfast by way of the Long Bridge (the only crossing of the Lagan until Ormeau Bridge was built some years later). They also built a pleasant smaller house, at Doagh in Co. Antrim, which was named Fisherwick Lodge and used as the headquarters of the Doagh Hunt.

Though Donegall's income was by any standards a large one, his debts were so enormous—a quarter of a million, equal to fifteen or more in modern currency—that he had to pay a large part of it in interest. He also had large bills from the lawyers, for he refused to pay many of his early gambling debts on the grounds that the claims were fraudulent, with the result that he became involved in a great many lawsuits. Indeed he became so notorious for not paying debts of any kind that he appeared in print in a satirical tale published in 1821 as the 'Marquis of Done-'em-all'. One persistent creditor, a London moneylender who had bought up many of Donegall's bonds cheaply, actually turned up in Belfast to enforce payment by having the marquis's possessions seized by the sheriff and sold. He was outwitted, however, for the sheriffs of Antrim and Down were reluctant to do their duty against the local landlord and, when they did, local juries found that Edward May and others appeared to have prior claims. It seems that Donegall's houses and farms were stocked entirely with other people's possessions.

Things went on like this until 1818, when the eldest son and heir Lord Belfast came of age, an event which was celebrated with great rejoicing. No one was more glad than Donegall himself, who had been promising his creditors that as soon as it happened he would make an arrangement with his son to raise the money to clear the estate of debt. The occasion for this was to be Lord Belfast's marriage to a daughter of the sixth earl of Shaftesbury. A week before the ceremony was due to take place, Shaftesbury received an anonymous letter telling him that the Donegalls had never been properly married and that Lord Belfast and his brothers were therefore illegitimate. When Shaftesbury investigated he found that the charge was true. It turned out that when Anna May, illegitimate and under age, had been hurriedly married to young Belfast in Marylebone parish church in 1795, in a ceremony performed by special licence, she ought to have had the consent not of her natural father (who was only too willing) but of a guardian appointed by the courts. Without that consent the marriage was illegal.

Anna marchioness of Donegall as a gypsy fortune-teller, with her infant son, Mrs May and Miss May, after the painting by J. J. Masquerier R.A., 1801 (Ulster Museum).

The news created a tremendous sensation, both in Belfast and elsewhere. The new heir, Arthur Chichester (later the first Lord Templemore), Donegall's nephew and the owner of Ballymacarrett, behaved very decently but seemed certain to inherit despite the attempts of the Donegalls to prove the validity of the marriage in the courts. All hope of a new settlement which would pay off Donegall's debts was abandoned along with the Shaftesbury match. In the end, after three years, the situation was saved by a retrospective change in the marriage law—a change brought about by the Donegall case. In vain Arthur Chichester petitioned parliament and the king against an Act that would deprive him of his unexpected inheritance. The new settlement was signed at last in 1822, when Lord Belfast married a new bride, Harriet Butler, daughter of the earl of Glengall.

Belfast was one of the very few provincial towns anywhere in the British Isles, and the only one in Ireland, to be owned entirely by one family. Until the middle of the nineteenth century, when the boundary was greatly extended to include Ballymacarrett on the Co. Down side of the Lagan, the town lay entirely within the Donegall estate in Co. Antrim. The Donegalls also owned Ballynafeigh on the Co. Down side, which contained Ormeau. Their influence on the growth and development of the town was naturally very great, especially during the latter part of the eighteenth century when the population had more than doubled to its 1800 total of over 20,000. The first marquis, though an absentee, had carefully planned and controlled all new building by granting leases which obliged tenants to build houses of uniform height and of good materials. He had also provided fine public buildings such as St Anne's church and the Exchange and Assembly Rooms at his own expense, and had generously donated land for the Poor House, the White Linen Hall, churches and other buildings, as well as paying £60,000 to complete the Lagan canal. Other major developments, such as much-needed improvements to the harbour were—like the Poor House and the Linen Hall—the result of activity by the leading citizens. The corporation—thirteen burgesses appointed by Donegall who chose one of his nominees as sovereign—did not count for much in the running of the town. Its main function, until the Reform Act of 1832 gave the vote to a large number of citizens, was to elect Belfast's MPs, who were always Donegall's relatives or nominees.

George Augustus, second marquis of Donegall (1769–1844), after the painting by J. J. Masquerier R.A., 1800 (Ulster Museum).

The second marquis continued his father's policy of providing land for public purposes—the Academical Institution in 1810, the Fever Hospital in 1815, the Commercial Buildings in 1819, the gasworks in 1822, for all of which he performed the opening ceremony, using the same silver trowel. His name usually headed the list of subscribers too, though more as an incentive to others than as a contributor (his £600 subscription to the Academical Institution, of which he was president for life, was never paid). In fact he gained a good reputation for treating the town generously so far as he could afford to, especially during his first twenty years or so. He was much less generous in his later years, not because he was less good-natured but because his power to help was more limited.

The reason for this was the settlement he and his son made in 1822. For years Donegall had been renewing leases at the same rents in return for cash. Now, in order to clear the estate of his debts, over £200,000 was to be raised by granting leases for ever at the existing rents (in most cases rather low ones) in return for ready money. Under this arrangement almost all the ground of Belfast—both as it then was and as it was to become—was granted away during the next few years, along with thousands of acres in Antrim and Donegal. So long as the rents were paid, the owners of these leases could practically do as they liked. All control by the landowner over the future growth of the town, its planning, appearance and architecture, was thus removed. Whereas Georgian Belfast had been the creation of the Donegalls, its development into a major Victorian city owed little to their guidance.

Fisherwick Lodge, Doagh, Co. Antrim (Ulster Museum).

Selling perpetual leases proved so tempting a way of raising money that Donegall and his son went on doing it long after the original target had been reached. Instead of £217,000 at least £330,000 was raised, of which Lord Belfast got his share. Though an enormous sum was thus taken out of the value of the estate, at least the income would no longer be burdened with the debts that had plagued Donegall for the whole of his adult life, and his successor would be free of both the debts and the lawsuits arising from them. Curiously enough, but not surprisingly, that was not the way it worked out. By the middle of the 1830s so much of Donegall's income was under the control of receivers appointed by his creditors that he could not even afford to keep up his subscriptions to local charities, and he remained in this situation until his death at Ormeau in 1844. Then something even more curious came to light: the third marquis discovered that the debts supposed to have been paid off in the 1820s were still owing. Somehow the father had managed to squander the money in other ways, and to conceal the fact from his son, who in the meantime had run up considerable debts of his own.

Exactly what Donegall did with all the money—in the ten years before 1832, when the sales of leases stopped, he must have gone through at least half a million—is a mystery. Normal expenditure for someone in his position could be heavy, of course: six younger sons must have been expensive to educate and provide livings for, and he had also had to spend money on cultivating the voters of Carrickfergus. He could better afford to indulge his passion for hunting and horse-racing (there are ballads about the lavish hospitality at Fisherwick Lodge during this period), and he owned a yacht called *Zoe* which he raced (and no doubt backed with heavy wagers) at local regattas. The largest single item of extraordinary expenditure that we know of, however, was the rebuilding of Ormeau.

Ormeau House from across the River Lagan, c. 1832, artist unknown (Ulster Museum).

Up till 1822 the Donegalls' main residence was a modest country-style house known as Ormeau Cottage. In the following year work began on a much larger and more imposing building in the Tudor style which was to be known as Ormeau House. It was designed by a distinguished young Irish architect, William Vitruvius Morrison, and built by local craftsmen. Later valued for rates at what was then the large sum of £100, the house and its attached offices had a ground area of more than 20,000 square feet, a dozen principal bedrooms, as well as a dozen others, a banqueting hall, a long gallery and other fine public rooms. The building and furnishing of such a large house benefited local merchants, suppliers, tradesmen and shopkeepers considerably. We know from the agent's accounts that most of the materials and furnishings were bought in Belfast, only such things as stained glass (supplied from Dublin) and the latest kind of patent lamps (from London) being purchased elsewhere. The famous Lisburn firm of Coulson's supplied the linen sheets and tablecloths.

The establishment at Ormeau also provided employment for a large number of people, from professional men such as lawyers down to grooms and stable boys, and many upstairs and downstairs staff in the house itself (where instead of running water there were two dozen leather buckets to be filled and carried). Apart from those permanently employed as servants, many other Belfast people depended on Donegall's custom. Payments connected with horses are prominent in the accounts. In the 1820s Donegall's bill for forage alone from Samuel Rea, a provision merchant in York Street, was running at £1,600 a year. Joseph Redfern of Castle Street, 'saddler and harness maker (and military accoutrement maker)' as he called himself in the directory, had considerable demands too. Horse doctoring was another recurrent expense: Mrs Martha Gill of Talbot Street, listed in 1824 as one of the three veterinary surgeons in the town, was paid nearly £60 on one occasion. Large amounts were paid to Gordon's, the wine merchants in Castle Street—nearly £2,000 during the three years 1823–26—as well as other sums to wine merchants in Dublin. The new chimneys at Ormeau apparently needed the expert attention of John Kearney of North Street, 'smoke doctor', whose bill for £50 was paid in 1824. Clearly a great landowner who was resident and spent his money freely was an economic as well as a social asset to the town. He could also be a liability to the local shopkeepers if, like Donegall, he ran up large bills and was slow to pay.

Ormeau House in 1832, after the drawing by J. Molloy (Ulster Museum).

The last years of the second marquis's life at Belfast were clouded by renewed financial anxieties, which not only hampered his free-spending personal habits but also led to disputes with the citizens over the buying out of the family's remaining rights as owners of the soil. The population of the town had shot up to nearly 50,000 by 1830, and its physical growth led to the area under the control of the corporation being extended in 1836 to encompass one and a half square miles. By 1841 the inhabitants numbered over 70,000, not including the expanding suburb of Ballymacarrett. An improvement in the water supply, never very satisfactory, became desperately urgent, and it was felt that the Donegalls (particularly the heir to the title) drove a hard bargain before agreeing to sell to the new Water Commissioners. By this time, they had lost political control of Belfast. Though Lord Arthur Chichester did indeed gain one of the two seats in the first election after the Reform Act, he did so only by enduring a rowdy contest, and only after what the *Northern Whig* described as the 'farce' of his mother the marchioness going around the town to woo the shopkeepers on his behalf. Finally, in 1840 the reform of the Irish municipal corporations deprived the family of its control in local government, replacing the old sovereign and burgesses by an elected council. The last sovereign, Donegall's nephew, failed even to get a seat.

He himself remained popular, however, and not only because his folly in financial matters was to the advantage of his tenants. As someone remarked, he had 'a mild and gentle disposition and peculiarly pleasing suavity of manner'; while Dr Henry Cooke, the not so mild and gentle presbyterian divine, related how when he himself was ill on one occasion Donegall had called every day to enquire about him. Donegall had always patronised the lighter social amenities of the town as well as the more serious good causes

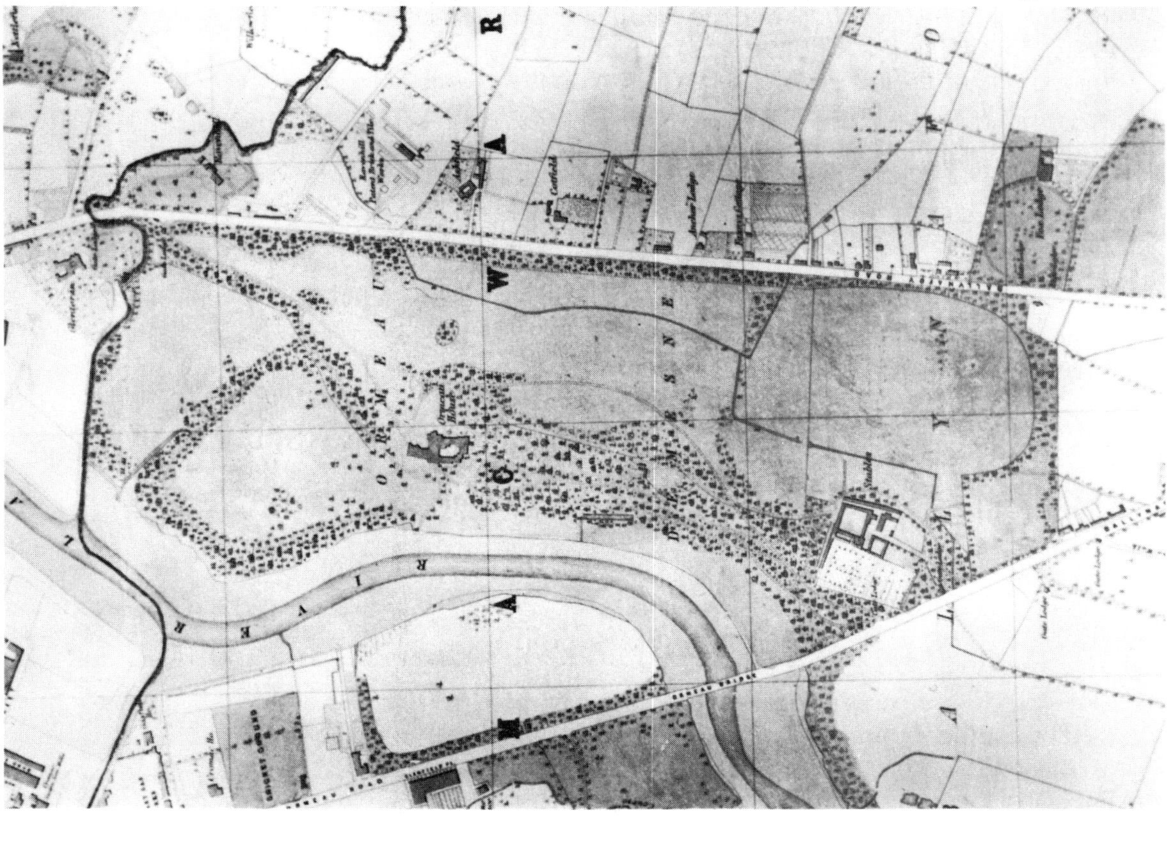

Ormeau demesne, from a map of Belfast published in 1864.

(when the first public baths were opened at Peter's Hill in 1805 he made them fashionable with the respectable citizens, and was a regular attender of the theatre). Even as an old man he found new sporting interests by encouraging the formation of the town's first cricket and rowing clubs. The expressions of regret at his death appear to have been genuine, though a proposal to erect a statue by public subscription never came to anything.

After the death of the second marquis the Donegalls left Ormeau. For the next ten years or so it was occupied by Thomas Verner, the last sovereign of Belfast, who acted as agent for his cousin the third marquis. The new Lord Donegall made his career in the army and at court, and while he occasionally visited Belfast had no desire—and unlike his father was not obliged— to live on his estates. The size of those estates was in any case soon to be drastically reduced. Whereas the Donegall lands in the north were heavily burdened by inherited debts, elsewhere in Ireland landowners were going bankrupt because of the potato famine, which made tenants unable to pay their rents. In order to replace debt-ridden owners with landlords who had money to spend on improving their property, an act was passed in 1849 appointing a body of three commissioners—usually known as the Encumbered Estates Court—with powers to take over estates and sell as much as was needed to pay off the debts, giving the new owners a clear title guaranteed by parliament. The Donegall estate was one of the first, and one of the largest, to be dealt with.

Since most of the tenants—all but 100 of the 800 in Belfast—already had perpetuity leases at low rents, a great deal had to be sold before

Frederick Richard, earl of Belfast (1827–1853) by R. Rothwell, R.H.A. (Ulster Museum).

the slate was wiped clean. Practically the whole town, even as greatly enlarged by another boundary extension in 1853, was bought by the tenants or by wealthy speculators. The only two substantial areas that remained in Donegall's hands after 1855 were Ormeau demesne and the deerpark on the slopes of the Cave Hill, and the total rent he got from Belfast was only £1,300. The Donegall estate was to remain one of the largest in the country, if perpetuities were included, but after two and a half centuries this was the end of their ownership of Belfast.

By the time the court had finished its work the Donegalls had also lost their only son. Frederick Richard, earl of Belfast, was a romantic figure, young, talented (he wrote poetry and composed music, including a waltz for Queen Victoria's visit to Ireland), handsome in the way the Victorians liked, and keen on popular education (the lectures he gave to raise money for a working men's library were published in 1852). His death of scarlatina at Naples in 1853 at the age of twenty-five was a dreadful blow to his father. In Belfast a statue—the original 'Black Man'—was erected to him in College Square East, in front of the Academical Institution. The remaining child, Harriet, in 1857 married the eldest son and heir of the seventh earl of Shaftesbury, the great reformer. The Shaftesbury alliance, which had fallen through at the last moment in 1819, thus came about in the next generation. The devout Shaftesbury often disapproved of his daughter-in-law's worldliness and lack of decorum, but the marriage eventually restored the ailing fortunes of his family, for on the death of her brother Harriet Chichester became heiress to the whole of her father's estate except Islandmagee. When the third marquis died in 1883 the Donegall property thus became part of the Shaftesbury estates.

Oddly enough, it was only after he had got rid of Belfast that the third marquis became interested in living there. His first wife's sister had built a new house in Tipperary, designed in the fashionable Scottish baronial style by W. H. Lynn, the junior partner in the Belfast

Gate Lodge, Belfast Castle, 1874, by J. J. Phillips (Ulster Museum).

firm of Lanyon & Lynn. After marrying again in 1862 Lord Donegall decided to abandon Ormeau and its 'ill-constructed residence' as he called it, and build a new one in the deerpark. Lynn designed the present Belfast Castle, which was constructed between 1867 and 1870 on what were then the bare slopes of Cave Hill. The Chapel of the Resurrection was built in the grounds, as a memorial to the late earl of Belfast and as a new mausoleum for the family.

Belfast Castle, 1874, by J. J. Phillips (Ulster Museum).

The demesne at Ormeau was let during the 1860s, while the empty house went to rack and ruin. In 1865 plans were made by a well-known English landscape architect to turn its 175 acres into a garden suburb of substantial villas with large gardens. Fortunately for the ordinary citizens of the ever-expanding and unhealthy town of Belfast, the plan was not pursued. Instead, in 1869 the land was let to the town council for £10 an acre, and the council wisely decided to make most of it into Belfast's first public park (the Botanic Gardens were not acquired until 1895). Ormeau House and its outbuildings were razed to the ground and no trace of them remains. Following the example of towns in England, the council financed the project by selling part of the demesne for building (where Park Road and North and South Parade now are). The remainder, let for grazing at first, was leased to Ormeau Golf Club in 1892.

The revived interest in his family's connection with Belfast which had led Lord Donegall to build the new Castle was continued by his daughter and by his grandson the ninth earl of Shaftesbury. Though little of Belfast itself remained in their hands, their estate in Co. Antrim was still large enough to be worth visiting every year and was made easier to visit by improvements in transport. Perhaps, too, the growth of Belfast into one of the major cities of the kingdom made the connection interesting, particularly since there had never been any rival of a similar rank to them as local patrons. For their part, the city fathers and others in Belfast at the turn of the century welcomed aristocratic patrons who could give a lead and act as figureheads but who no longer had any real power, just as the city of Liverpool welcomed the active interest of the earls of Derby during the same period. The Shaftesburys not only did what was expected of them by supporting local charities, opening the Castle grounds for garden fetes and heading the subscription list for the new cathedral; the ninth earl in 1907 became lord mayor, and when the Queen's College was raised to the status of a university in the following year he became its first chancellor. His final act of patronage was to present the Castle and its grounds to the city in 1934.

To sum up, then, the Donegalls, who had established Belfast and contributed in many ways to its early development, played little or no part in its expansion into a great industrial city—except perhaps by disappearing from the scene at the right time. The interest of a single great landowner, however wise and paternal, could probably never have achieved as much as the self-interest of a large number of independent citizens. (It is interesting to note that the Templemores who owned Ballymacarrett, after making elaborate plans in the early 1850s to develop it themselves, later gave up this kind of investment and settled for a steady fixed income from ground rents). As it was, the astonishing extravagance of the second marquis put the whole matter out of the question for the Donegalls. In the end only their social importance remained. Even presbyterian Belfast loved a lord, especially if he was no longer a landlord.

3. 'Linenopolis': the rise of the textile industry

Emily Boyle

In 1750 Belfast was a small town with little importance for the Irish textile industry. By the outbreak of the First World War, however, it had been transformed into the largest linen producing centre not only in Ireland but in the world. The change in Belfast was caused, as was the case with many towns in the British Isles, by the coming of the Industrial Revolution.

In the middle of the eighteenth century, linen, the most common textile manufactured in Ireland, was not produced in towns or factories, but made domestically, in rural areas. It went hand in hand with agriculture: the family grew flax along with its foodstuffs, the wife and children prepared it and spun the yarn, and the husband wove the yarn into cloth. The woven cloth was taken to one of the brown linen markets where it was bought by bleachers for finishing, then exported to England, the main market, and elsewhere.

Though linen making was concentrated in Ulster, and remained

Engraving by William Hincks (1783), showing the female members of the family spinning, reeling and boiling flax yarn (Ulster Museum).

so, the opening up of new overseas markets—especially in South America—encouraged people in the other provinces—particularly Connacht, to turn to linen making as a means of boosting the family income. Irish linen was of a fine quality, and was used for such things as sheets, tablecloths, and clothing. The profitable export trade was controlled by merchants operating through Dublin. However, in the second half of the eighteenth century the bleachers of the Lagan valley gradually built up direct links with English merchants, sending their linens through Belfast. This brought about an important shift in the trading pattern. By 1783 Belfast's linen exports had grown to such an extent that the bleachers decided to build a hall in which white linens could be bought and sold. £10,000 was raised by public subscription, and in 1785, amid much ceremony and acclaim, the prestigious White Linen Hall was opened. Its symbolic significance can not have been lost on many, least of all the Dublin merchants.

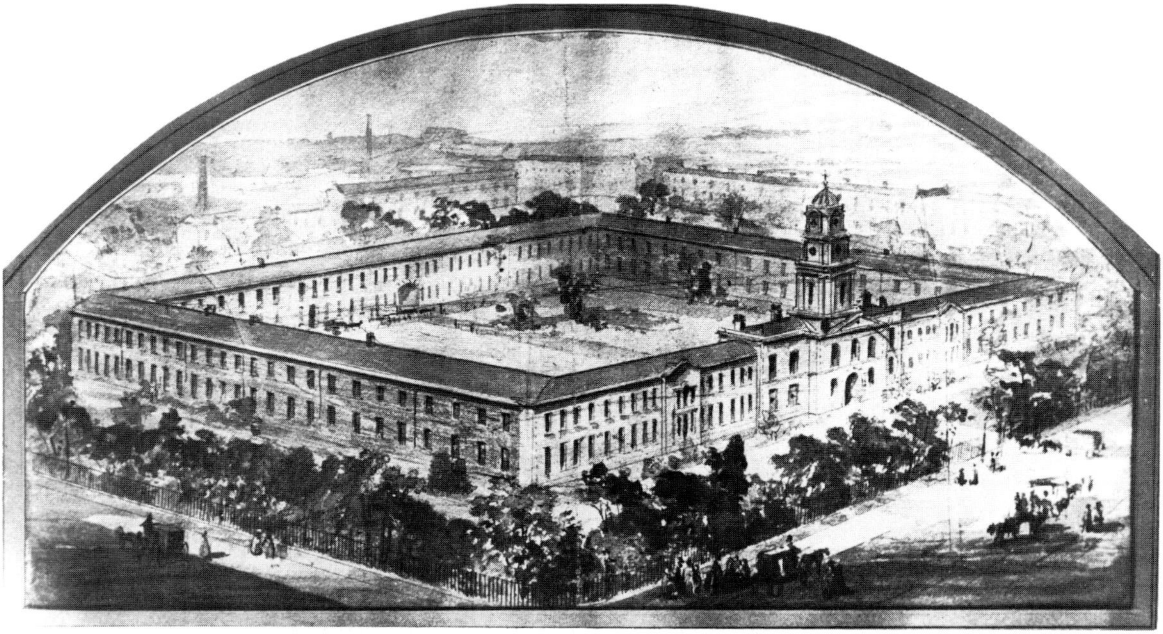

The White Linen Hall, built in 1783, was evidence of the increasing importance of the town to the linen trade (Hogg Collection, Ulster Museum).

However, some years before the White Linen Hall was first mooted, the seeds had been sown for the transformation of Belfast from a market town and linen exporting centre into a large industrial city. Ironically, the route for this transformation was not a direct one from the domestic production of linen in the town's hinterland to its industrialised production inside the city's boundaries. Rather it took a diversion by way of the cotton industry, which grew out of an experiment started in Belfast's Poor House in 1778.

In that year the Belfast Charitable Committee decided that the children of the Poor House could be usefully employed spinning cotton by hand. Nicholas Grimshaw, a committee member, provided a carding machine and spinning wheel for the operation. About a year later Robert Joy and Thomas McCabe offered to install machinery which would enable them to carry on their spinning on a larger scale. This offer was readily accepted and so, in effect, part of the Belfast Poor House became the town's first spinning mill. By 1780 the operation employed ninety.

From this unusual beginning the Belfast cotton spinning industry expanded rapidly because the cost of mill spinning drastically undercut the cost of hand spinning. Furthermore, although Belfast cotton spinners experienced certain disadvantages vis à vis their Lancashire rivals, they were protected from this competition by a high tariff barrier.

By 1820 over 2,000 people were employed in about fifteen cotton mills spread over the city and out as far as Lisburn, Bangor and Larne. The centre of the industry, however, was the Smithfield area. Here, John McCracken's mill employed 200, operating 14,000 spindles, while the workforce of McCrum, Lepper and Co. was 300. Their mill, which was sited behind the Artillery Barracks, was 200 feet long, 40 feet wide and 5 storeys high—a massive structure for the time. Another mill in Winetavern Street was 70 feet long, 36 feet wide and 5 storeys high, with 5,364 spindles and 24 carding machines. In 1815

Portrait of Thomas Mulholland (1756–1830), who built the first flax spinning mill in Belfast (attributed to Samuel Hawksett, Ulster Museum).

this mill was bought by Thomas Mulholland, who later acquired one in Francis Street, and in 1822 built another in Henry Street, becoming one of the largest manufacturers in the town. He was to play a vital role in the development of Belfast's textile industry.

Cotton spinning in Belfast reached a peak around 1825–6, when more than 3,500 people were employed in over twenty mills. However, a combination of circumstances brought about upheaval in both the linen and cotton industries and led to the Belfast cotton industry's swift decline. Firstly, the tariff barrier which protected Irish cotton yarn from direct competition with British yarn was lifted in 1824. In the same year James Kay of Preston patented his wet spinning process for spinning fine linen yarns. Within a few years Marshall's of Leeds had successfully adopted this process for commercial purposes. Furthermore, the United Kingdom cotton industry began to slide into a deep recession in 1826. On top of all this, in the summer of 1828 Mulholland's big, new Henry Street mill was burnt down.

Before rebuilding it the Mulhollands looked into the possibility of adapting it for spinning flax rather than cotton. Thomas had recently noticed that large amounts of flax were being exported to be machine spun in England, and that equally large amounts of linen yarn came back, on the Liverpool steamer, to be handwoven into cloth. Impressed with the logic of establishing a flax spinning mill in Belfast he and his partner John Hind took a trip to Leeds 'to inquire into the state of the (flax) trade there', and look into the idea's

York Street Flaxspinning Mill, by J. H. Burgess (Hall's *Ireland*, London, 1842).

feasibility. Meanwhile, Andrew and St Clair Mulholland, Thomas's brothers, toured York and Lancaster to find out as much as possible about mechanical flax spinning. During 1828–9, as a technical experiment, the firm established 1000 flax spindles in its Francis Street Mill. These worked efficiently and so the mill, which became known as the York Street Mill, was rebuilt to spin flax. It was opened in 1830 and contained some 8,000 flax spinning spindles.

The operation was an outstanding success, and there was a rush amongst cotton spinners to adapt their mills for spinning flax. Not only cotton spinners. Belfast's business community smelt success, and capital and entrepreneurial talent were attracted from all quarters. Robert Thompson, who built the Wolfhill Mill, was a bleacher, William Ewart, who built the Crumlin Road Mill, was originally a cotton manufacturer and merchant, Robert McKibbin, founder of the Connswater Mill, was a doctor, and Edmund Grimshaw, acting in a spirit Nicholas would have approved of, converted the Mossley printworks to flax spinning. In 1834 there were only marginally fewer people spinning flax than cotton. The trend continued and by 1850 only four mills in Belfast spun cotton against twenty-nine spinning flax.

The mechanisation of flax spinning in and around Belfast, and to a

Inside John Chartre's Mill, by J. H. Burgess (Hall's *Ireland*, London 1842). It was described by a contemporary as one of the most 'elegant' operating.

lesser extent in the other towns of the north-east of the country, spelt economic disaster not only for the handspinners, who simply could not produce yarn as cheaply as the mills, but also for handloom weavers living in the outlying regions of Ulster and Connacht, who did not have easy access to the mills, and found it increasingly difficult to procure yarn for weaving. Many of these weavers moved into the north-eastern area in order to be closer to the mills. At the same time many of the former handspinners living in the vicinity of the mills turned to weaving.

In these circumstances mill spinners could rely upon a plentiful supply of handloom weavers to make up their yarns for very little reward. They were, therefore, in no hurry to introduce powerloom weaving into the industry. Furthermore, although powerlooms could weave the coarser types of linen, such as that for sacking and canvas, they were still not suitable for weaving the finer counts of yarn. For these reasons the weaving sector of the industry in Ireland remained unindustrialized until the middle part of the century.

Linen handloom weaving continued long after flax spinning had become mechanised. At the end of the nineteenth century 2,000 handlooms were still being operated in Ulster (engraving by William Hincks, 1783, Ulster Museum).

It was the devastation wrought by the Famine on both the number of skilled weavers and the land holding system that sustained them, forcing up their wages, which eventually stimulated the flax spinners of Belfast into a more active search for an alternative. At the same time modifications were being made to Britain's coarse linen powerlooms which made them more suited to the finer Irish linens, and by 1850 two Belfast firms had begun powerloom weaving. Even so its diffusion was slow, and by 1862 there were still less than 3,000 powerlooms operating in the Belfast area.

However, the outbreak of the American Civil War in 1861 brought about dramatic changes. Northern ships blockaded the ports of the Confederate States of America, virtually cutting off the supply of raw cotton to Britain, starving the Lancashire cotton mills of work and creating a dearth of cotton goods on the world market. Linens took their place. Demand soared and the Belfast industrialists responded enthusiastically, rapidly increasing their capacity for both spinning and weaving. The number of flax spinning spindles operating in and around Belfast increased from less than 500,000 in 1862, to 724,000

Powerloom linen weaving was slow to be adopted in Belfast; by 1850 only two firms in the city used powerlooms (W. A. McCutcheon, Ulster Museum).

in 1868, and the number of powerlooms rose from under 3,000 to nearly 9,000. Seven new weaving factories were opened, including Lawnbrook, Bain's Place, Loopbridge, Cupar Street and Brookfield, and two firms became integrated spinning and weaving concerns.

Existing firms added to their plant. For example, John Hind and Co. of Durham Street spent £75,000 between 1862 and 1868 building four large mills and a weaving factory. A powerloom factory was added to the Smithfield Mill, and William Ewart and Son added a new mill and a weaving factory to their already sizeable plant. Even so Ewarts had such a volume of orders that they brought their employees back to work, illegally, in the evenings. Although the Factory Inspectorate was aware of what was happening it could do very little about it; as one indignant inspector reported in 1870:

> Messrs Ewart and Sons have repeatedly been reported for serious infringements in their spinning mill and . . . have always been dealt with very leniently. . . . What makes the case worse is that Mr William Ewart junior is a magistrate and alderman.

The profits made by the Belfast linen lords in these years were vast. One contemporary spoke of 'profitable returns of well nigh fabulous percentage', and claimed that for two years running one firm's profits 'equalled the value of the entire premises and plant'. Certainly, Gunning and Campbell, flaxspinners of Mossley Mill just outside Belfast, saw their profits rise from under £7,000 in 1861, to over £21,000 in 1864.

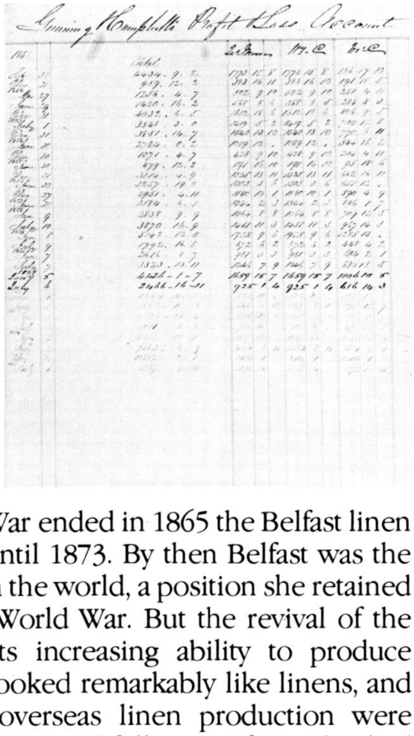

Profit and Loss account for Gunning and Campbell 1851–1865 (Public Record Office of Northern Ireland).

Although the American Civil War ended in 1865 the Belfast linen industry continued to prosper until 1873. By then Belfast was the largest linen producing centre in the world, a position she retained until the outbreak of the First World War. But the revival of the British cotton industry, with its increasing ability to produce inexpensive cotton goods that looked remarkably like linens, and the rapid industrialisation of overseas linen production were undermining Belfast's position. Demand fell. Soon, firms that had overextended their activities during the halcyon days of the sixties were finding themselves with liquidity problems. At the end of 1875 two such companies, William Spotten and Co., and Lowry, Valentine and Kirk, both of which had been in financial trouble since May 1874, when payment on their shares had been suspended, went bankrupt. Both firms were hopelessly insolvent. These collapses brought others in their wake, including Malcolmson and Co., of

'Waterford, Belfast and half a dozen other places', Samuel E. Broadbent of Cogry, and the Bedford Street Weaving Company. This spate of failures rocked the confidence of the industry, but worse was to come. In the mid 1880s there was another run of bankruptcies, headed by the collapse of the mighty John Hind and Co. 'one of the oldest, largest and most respectable firms in the spinning trade'. This disaster was precipitated by a court case that is possibly unparalleled in business history. The problem began in 1854 when John Hind, a founding partner, died. In his will he asked for his share in the firm to be sold, and the proceeds divided amongst his sizeable family. However, at that time the linen industry was going through a temporary recession and no buyer could be found. The trustees of the will, John Hind's two sons, John and James, then suggested that they should buy the share at a price established by an independent arbitrator. The rest of the family readily agreed and this was done. The business flourished until 1878, when one William Stables, acting on behalf of the children of Francis, John Hind's youngest daughter, entered into a lawsuit in Chancery against the trustees of John Hind deceased and the survivors of his family, including the children's parents. Stables alleged that John and James Hind as trustees had acted illegally in buying up the property and claimed for the children a share of the profits made by the firm from 1854–79 with compound interest. These amounted to several hundred thousand pounds. The case was eventually heard in 1881 and the verdict went in favour of the plaintiff. For many months after the hearing a hoard of accountants were employed in estimating the amount owed to the children. The result of the proceedings was that the firm simply could not bear the costs and went into liquidation, bringing down several smaller firms, mainly from outside Belfast.

1898 witnessed yet another round of bankruptcies. These included the Belfast Flax Spinning Company, the Ligoniel Spinning Company, the Co. Down Flax Spinning and Weaving Company and Cogry Flax Spinning Company. The condition of the linen industry in and around Belfast, poor as it was, did not compare with the lot of firms in more peripheral areas. Here, the problems were heightened by higher transport costs and the numerous small disadvantages entailed in being distant from the centre of the trade. Business became increasingly unreliable and companies in Limavady, Keady, Castleblayney, Buncrana, Coleraine, Ballymoney and Emyvale went into liquidation, leaving the industry even more concentrated in the Belfast area. Even when the fortunes of the industry began to pick up in the first decade of the twentieth century it never recovered this broad geographical base.

The linen entrepreneurs fought hard to alleviate the problems of the industry. They introduced more efficient means of production. In flax preparation the improved piecing out system of roughing was

Roughing was the most unhealthy operation in the linen industry. Few roughers spent long at the job without their health being affected. (Welch Collection, Ulster Museum).

developed, and new hackling machinery was introduced. (Roughing and hackling, known collectively as sorting, involve the combing of the flax to ensure the strands of fibre are not tangled.) In the spinning rooms the machinery was speeded up and the spinning frames increased in size to hold 260 rather than 124 spindles. Again, the use of powerlooms was constantly being extended.

In the face of reduced demand from markets such as Europe, which was developing its own linen industry, and the West Indies, where cotton was superseding linen, the merchants increased their selling efforts in rapidly developing areas of the British Empire such as Australia, Canada, New Zealand and South Africa. Their marketing had never lacked ingenuity, not to say plain guile; for instance when exporting to South America, which mostly used continental linens, the city's merchants copied continental packaging—Prussian eagles abounded—and exported much of their produce through Hamburg. They also sought out new uses for linen. These included clothing for that new pastime of the rich—motoring; and fine mesh underwear, tastefully advertised as being 'eminently suitable for wearing next to the body'.

Their efforts were not in vain. In the first decade of the twentieth century the demand for Irish linen began to pick up, and with it came an increase in Belfast's capacity to produce it. The number of spindles in operation rose by 5 per cent between 1900–13, and the number of powerlooms by 18 per cent. Several new weaving factories were built, including Dunmurry, Donegall and Victoria. By the outbreak of World War One the Belfast linen industry was the most developed in the world. Furthermore, the industry was prospering, and the immediate outlook was extremely bright: government demand for linen as a war material—for use in kit bags, tents, and even aeroplanes—was likely to be considerable. The linen lords looked forward to a period of prosperity.

A wetspinning room in a Belfast mill (Hogg collection, Ulster Museum). The atmosphere here was stiflingly hot and humid and the floor always wet. Workers' clothes often became saturated with spray from the spindles.

Whilst owners and managers were wrestling with the problems of the fluctuating fortunes of the industry, most of the workforce were faced with much more personal and pressing problems: coping with the often damaging effects of linen work on their health, and trying to make ends meet. The workforce was made up predominantly of women and children. Employers preferred them because they were cheap—their wages never amounting to more than about half those of skilled men. They themselves usually worked out of economic necessity. In 1911 one old mill-hand explained:

> When you were eight you were old enough to work. . . .If you got married you kept on working. Your man didn't get enough for a family. You worked till your baby came and went back as soon as you could . . . and then you counted the years till your child could be a half timer.

The conditions in which these people worked were among the most unhealthy imaginable. For almost all types of linen spinning and weaving the atmosphere needed to be very hot and humid, even more so than for cotton production. In the wet spinning rooms, where the majority of children worked, the floors were always wet and the workers went barefoot. Clothes became saturated with the spray from the spindles. Children working in these conditions often developed lung diseases when they were very young. Concern was such that two special inquiries were conducted by the Factory Inspectorate. These showed that the children who worked in the Belfast linen mills had poorer stamina and were smaller than those working in cotton mills in Britain. (Though these reports did not directly lead to any changes, Belfast's employers had a creditable safety record and were generally quick to implement any required improvements in conditions.)

Conditions for weaving were as bad as those for spinning. They left workers particularly prone to diseases such as bronchitis. (Hogg Collection, Ulster Museum).

The weaving factories were little better. Here, humidity often reached within a degree or two of saturation point causing evaporation from the body to cease, forcing up body temperatures, leading to giddiness and lassitude. Furthermore, they were very vulnerable to bronchitis and similar illnesses, because after working in these stifling conditions all day they would step out into the cool evening air with their clothes and bodies still damp.

However, the most unhealthy conditions were experienced in the flax preparing departments, particularly in roughing and hackling. Here work was carried on 'in a continual cloud of dust composed of large and small particles of fibre'. The dust, known as 'pouce', gradually began irritating and drying up the worker's throat, after which it attacked the lungs causing violent spasms of coughing. This condition, called 'poucey', was the forerunner of the lethal 'mechanical phthisis'—a form of tuberculosis. In the flax preparing rooms the working life was short and the mortality rate high. In 1872 the average working life of someone employed in these processes, before they became unfit to work, or died, was only 16.8 years, and of every thousand at work thirty-one died. Nineteen years later nearly half the linen workers who died in Belfast were suffering from phthisis, and 90 per cent of them were under forty years old.

The only processes in the industry which did not require unhealthy conditions were yarn dressing, and the final stages, known as finishing and making up, which included linen lapping, embroidering and packaging. These jobs were usually carried on

Embroidering was seen as a more desirable occupation than spinning or weaving— but the pay was no better. (Hogg Collection, Ulster Museum).

separately from spinning and weaving, and were regarded as socially superior; as Nora Connolly O'Brien discovered when she first went to work in a making up wareroom in Belfast, where she was sharply rebuked by a fellow worker for thinking she was working in a factory. As Nora remarked:

> Gracious! How indignant she was. And she told me I was working in a wareroom; that factory workers were weavers, rope workers, tobacco workers. A wareroom was ever so much higher in the social scale than a factory.

Despite the social kudos attached to the making up processes, the wages here were no better than in other sectors of the industry, and these, for the majority, were very low indeed. For example, in 1855, when a four pound loaf of bread cost 7½d, a pound of meat cost 5½d and coal was 7½d per hundredweight, women and girls in the industry earned on average 5/6d, lads 3/3d and unskilled men 10/6d. By 1905 things had improved slightly. Whereas the price of a loaf of bread had fallen to 5½d, meat was about the same, and coal had risen to 10d per hundredweight, women and girls' wages averaged 9/-, lads 10/-, and unskilled men 17/- per week. Even so it has been estimated that unskilled men could only just have earned enough to keep a family of two adults and two children with 'minimum comfort'.

Several reasons can be suggested for this miserable level of wages. Firstly, there was the unskilled nature of the work, combined with the constant presence of a pool of unemployed people willing and able to do it. In addition, as has been mentioned, most of the workers were women and young people, who traditionally earned considerably less than adult men—even for doing the same job.

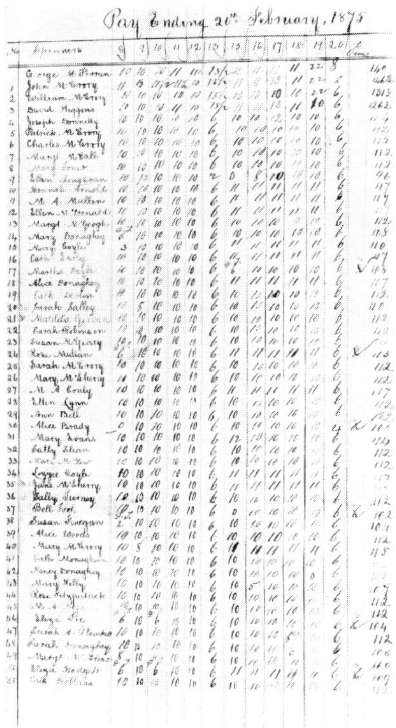
Pay Ending 20th February, 1875

Part of a typical page from a mill's wages book (Public Record Office of Northern Ireland). The figure in the right hand column is the wage, in old pence, for two five and a half day weeks.

Also, trade unionism among linen workers was weak. Although unions had made faltering inroads into the industry since the early 1870s, by 1910 less than 12 per cent of the workforce was organised, and those who were were represented by ten different unions. Nine of these catered for the sectional interests of the various skilled groups, and accounted for about 60 per cent of the union membership. Only the Textile Operatives of Ireland union was open to the whole of the industry, but it had a mere 2,500 members out of a total linen workforce of about 74,000 (throughout Ireland).

The final reason for the low earnings of the majority of linen workers is that they rarely attempted to challenge them. This was partly the result of the weakness and sectional structure of trade unionism, and partly a result of the economic stagnation of the last quarter of the nineteenth century. Attempts by the workers to improve their lot by industrial action were singularly unsuccessful. In 1872 roughers and sorters struck for five weeks for a 20 per cent increase—to no avail. In 1874 workers in forty-three mills went on strike for seven weeks in opposition to a cut in their wages—again to no avail. Other smaller strikes, in later years, met with similar results; indeed frequently the striking workers were replaced—either by other workers or by machines. Under the circumstances it is hardly surprising that the lower paid demonstrated little opposition. However not everyone was badly paid. Indeed the skilled workers, and particularly the overseers, were paid extremely well. In 1855 skilled men earned approximately 18/-, and overlookers 24/-per week. In 1905 this had risen to 23/- and 42/- per week respectively, enough for modest affluence.

In spite of the tribulations of the linen workers, the industry added significantly to the wealth of the city, and its role in Belfast's development cannot be overestimated. Without it the city might have remained a market town and port, for until the last quarter of the century linen was its only major industry and the people who flocked into 'Linenopolis', as Belfast became known, did so to work in the mills and factories.

Even by then, however, the circumstances which were to bring about the decline of the Belfast linen empire were in train. The industry had established itself at a time when cotton was not available. With its return to the world market and the increasing use of cotton in goods previously made of linen Belfast's position was undermined. Imaginative efforts on the part of producers followed by the Indian summer of the First World War extended the period of prosperity, however the industry went into deep recession soon after the war. This had much to do with the nature of linen itself. Expensive to produce and extremely durable, it was not suited to the world of rapidly changing fashion and mass produced clothing which emerged during the inter-war years. Though the industry did all in its power to adapt to changed times, the era of Belfast as a thriving textile town was over.

4. The development of the port

Robin Sweetnam

Though Belfast's port facilities were quite modest at the end of the eighteenth century, they were far from insignificant, as can be seen from James Williamson's map of the town, published in 1791. At the foot of High Street, at the mouth of the Farset river, the Town Dock had been extended down towards the low water line of the River Lagan, and the Hanover Quay had been constructed from the south side of the Dock up to the Long Bridge taking in, from the strand, the area now occupied by Marlborough and Princes Streets, which was then developed for commercial and residential use. Just north of the Town Dock a shallow creek gave access to the lime kiln at the foot of Waring Street. Further north again, at the end of the Fore Plantation, was William Ritchie's new shipyard, at the head of another small creek.

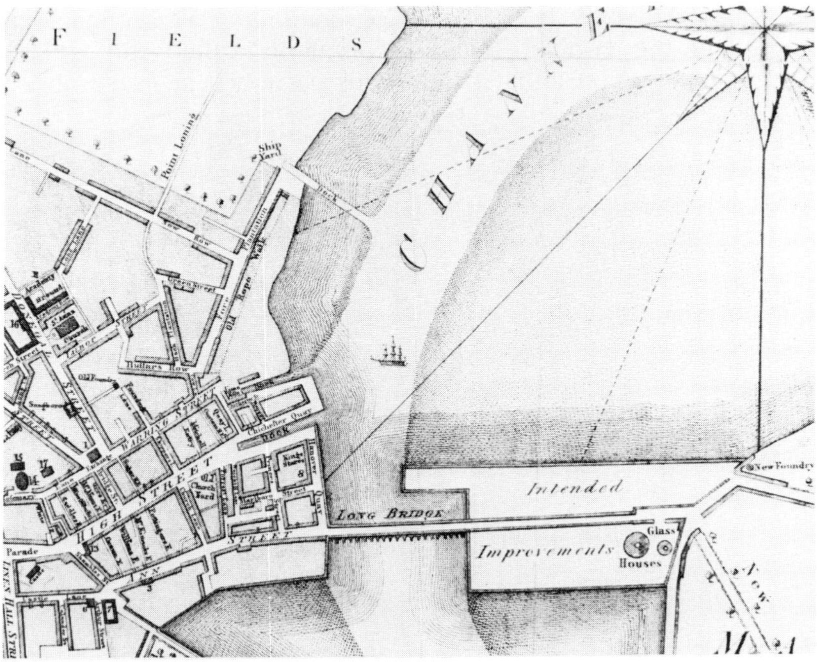

Part of James Williamson's Map of Belfast, 1791. The early 17th century 'Town Key' was at the mouth of the River Farset at the foot of High Street. Development of the port further up stream was effectively blocked by the completion of the Long Bridge in 1688.

At high water the open sea came right up to the quays and an uninterrupted view of the lough from the half-mile extent of the Long Bridge was one of the sights of the town. At low water, however, the berths in front of the quays dried out and the Lagan, less than two feet deep at midstream, could be seen making its tortuous way through sand and mud banks down to the deep waters of the Pool of Garmoyle, some three miles below the town. This made the landing of cargo an extremely difficult, slow and expensive business, as the shallowness of the river meant that even at spring tides only the smallest of vessels could come up to the quays without first lightening ship by discharging part of their cargo into small craft called gabbards.

The delay and additional costs occasioned by the poor approach to the town led the Chamber of Commerce in 1785 to present a petition to the Irish house of commons drawing attention to 'the great injury of Commerce and of your Petitioners' caused by the 'tedious and difficult' navigation up the channel, and requesting some £2,000 towards the cost of cutting a straight channel from the quay to Garmoyle across the tidal sloblands 'by means of which Vessels of a large Burthen would be enabled to pass up or down at high water in common tides'.

Characteristically, parliament did not agree to provide money, but gave what was to prove even more important, the transfer of responsibility for the control of the harbour from the impotent and unrepresentative town council to the merchant community who had a direct interest in its efficient management and development. By an Act of 1785 a new body, 'The Corporation for Preserving and Improving the Port of Belfast'—commonly called the Ballast Board—was formed; and it is significant that almost all its members

Part of a facsimile of the map of Belfast from *The History of the Town of Belfast* by George Benn, 1823. By the beginning of the 19th century, private quays had been built between the Long Bridge and the first sharp bend in the River Lagan. The berths at the quays dried out at low water and even at mid stream the river was only a few feet deep.

were successful merchants of the town and signatories to the original petition.

The new Board started enthusiastically, and did what they could within their limited income to remove the worst of the shoals in the channel, and, by making pilotage compulsory, reduce the frequent obstruction of the river by vessels which had run aground. The Board's main aim, however, was the acquisition of an area near the channel where a quay and ship repair facilities could be built. This proved difficult. At first the marquis of Donegall, who owned the foreshore, said that he would build the required docks himself, but with the final stages of the construction of the Lagan Navigation proving a continuing drain on his resources, he obviously had second thoughts and in 1795 granted the Board a ninety-nine year lease of some ten acres near Ritchie's shipyard. This was exactly what Belfast's merchant members wanted and almost immediately construction began on the town's first dry dock which, it was proudly announced, was 'capable of containing at one time three vessels of 200 tons each'. The dock is still in use today.

The provision of commercial quays was, however, felt to be beyond the resources of the Board at the time and this aspect of the port's development was left to individual merchants. In 1796 Narcissus Batt reclaimed land on the Co. Down foreshore just below the Long Bridge and built a quay. Here salt and vitriol works were established, adding to the industrial development at Ballymacarrett, where an iron foundry and glass works had already been built. Nearer the town David Tomb, in 1804, built the Donegall Quay between the Limekiln Dock at the foot of Waring Street and Ritchie's Dock to the north.

Helped by the completion of the Lagan Navigation to Lough

The Old Ballast Office, Donegall Quay, by A. C. Stannus, 1850 (Belfast Harbour Commissioners). Lanyon's Custom House now occupies the site where the old Ballast Office stood until 1854. The observatory on the roof gave the harbour master a clear view of the port and channel seawards.

Neagh in 1793, by the growth of the cotton industry and an increasing export of provisions from the farms of the town's hinterland, trade grew steadily. In 1786, the first full year after the Ballast Board had been set up, 772 ships totalling 34,287 tons burden had entered the port. Fourteen years later, whilst the number of vessels remained the same, the tonnage had risen to 55,268 tons reflecting the larger size of ship being employed; and by 1814 the figures were 1,159 ships totalling 90,486 tons, an increase in tonnage over the twenty-eight year period of 250 per cent.

Belfast's early success as a port, in spite of its poor access from the open sea, is at first sight remarkable. It had, however, several material points in its favour. Unlike all the other inlets on the Ulster coast, Belfast Lough had a wide, deep entrance, giving easy access to ships under sail, and the Pool of Garmoyle at its head provided a safe sheltered anchorage. The town itself, although built on poor ground, was strategically placed to handle the trade of the Lagan valley as the interior of the country was developed and land communications improved. Another factor was the industrious, self-reliant nature of the merchant community—as early as the 1680s nearly half the trade of Belfast was carried in Belfast owned ships, which traded from the Baltic to the West Indies, often captained by their merchant owners, from families such as the Pottingers, whose successful ventures helped lay the foundations of Belfast's future commercial prosperity.

The economic outlook at the beginning of the nineteenth century was favourable. The period saw the end of the worst of the political unrest which had had such an inhibiting effect on investment. Commercial confidence was regained, and, although local industries had to meet ever increasing competition from more highly developed areas in Great Britain, the trade of the port began to double and redouble every fifteen years, as the import of coal and raw materials rose to unprecedented heights and the export of linen and provisions soared.

However the fundamental problem of improving the approach to the port had yet to be tackled; for, in spite of the Board's efforts, the primitive 'bag and spoon' and hand dredging plant available to them had only marginally improved the depth of the river, and the larger vessels still had to lighten ship at Garmoyle before coming up to the quays to complete discharge. This not only involved the merchants in extra handling costs, but also seriously inconvenienced the customs officials who had to supervise all the handling of goods between ship and shore in an effort to see that no revenue duty was lost.

In 1814, with the prospect of peace with France in sight, both the Ballast Board and the Commissioners of Customs decided independently to seek advice on how best to improve the port. Successive schemes requiring a canal approach and lock gates were

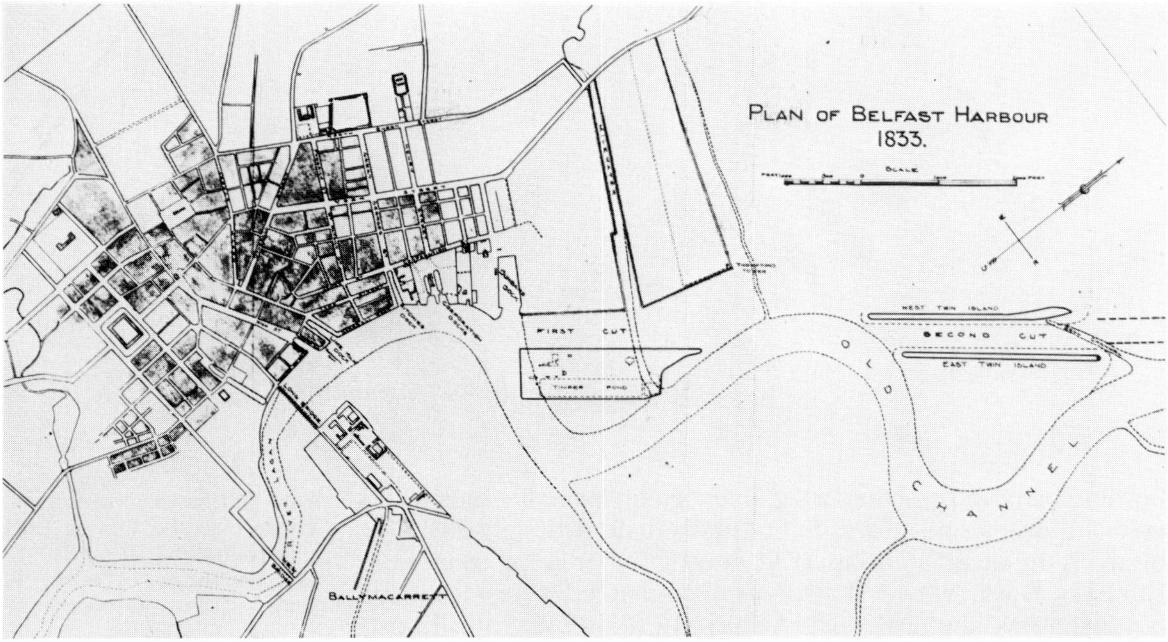

Plan of Belfast harbour in 1833 with First Cut (1841) and Second Cut (1849) superimposed (Belfast Harbour Commissioners). The opening of the 'Cuts' brought deep water up to the town and provided the central straight channel on which the modern harbour was developed.

rejected as too expensive, and it was not until 1830, when steam-powered dredgers had been introduced, that James Walker made the proposal, previously impracticable, that a straightened tidal channel leading to a deepened river in front of the town was economically feasible, and could be carried into effect in stages, as the need arose and financial resources allowed. Mr Walker's step by step ideas were very much in line with the thinking of the merchant community and were welcomed by the Board.

However the plans almost immediately ran into a powerful and determined opposition. A Bill, introduced into parliament to secure powers to improve the channel and to buy out the private quays, was bitterly opposed by the marquis of Donegall's nominees in the house on the grounds that the powers sought were too extensive to be vested in the Board. Donegall's intervention aroused deeply-felt anger, the *Northern Whig* recorded that 'the whole procedure admirably illustrates the base and villainous corruption on which our representative system is founded'. Further opposition came from Lord Templemore and others who wished to develop their lands at Ballymacarrett by constructing a channel on an alternative line across the Co. Down foreshore, and from the owners of the Co. Antrim foreshore, who initially sought compensation beyond the resources of the Board. However a compromise was eventually reached and Mr Walker's plan for a straightened tidal channel was accepted by all in 1837.

By then Belfast, despite its backward port facilities, was the 'First Town in Ireland for Trade', with the value of exports, mainly linen and provisions, exceeding imports by some £900,000 a year. The

View of Belfast harbour from the entrance to the Graving Dock Basin looking towards the Queen's Bridge (1849), by J. H. Burgess (Ulster Museum).

bustling harbour presented a sight very gratifying to the merchant's eye. The river's surface was full of movement, with lighters plying between the quays and Garmoyle, rafts of timber being taken from Dunbar's Dock, where it had been discharged overside, to be ponded above the now dilapidated Long Bridge, and small boats crossing between ship and shore. Steamers now accounted for a quarter of the tonnage thronging the port, and Belfast's thriving industry could boast of more steam-power than Dublin and Cork combined. At this point the need to carry out improvements was so pressing that the treasury consented, although with reluctance, to make a loan of £25,000 towards the cost of the first step of the Board's ambitious plans. William Dargan, the foremost contractor in Ireland, was engaged and completed the first cut in January 1841, providing a low water channel of at least nine feet in depth, adequate for most shipping, and, as a valuable by-product, creating the seventeen acre island which became known as 'Queen's Island'. The Board's next step, the purchase of all the privately owned quays, was completed by 1845, and the redevelopment of the harbour as a whole was now possible.

In 1846, despite the Famine and the depression in industry which threw thousands of Belfast weavers out of employment, traffic rose to over 500,000 tons, the shortfall in coal and raw materials more than balanced by the inflow of large quantities of food. To relieve unemployment, the Board hastily brought forward plans to make a second cut, extending the channel to Garmoyle, and Dargan again executed the work, which was opened as the 'Victoria Channel', amid scenes of jubilation, on 10 July 1849.

To provide deeper berths for the larger ships which could now come up the channel, a new Donegall Quay was built out in the river, across the front of all the older docks, which were then filled in to form the open areas we know as Victoria, Albert and Corporation Squares, and the smaller vessels, mainly colliers, were provided with

View of Belfast Harbour from the Custom House taken on the day of the opening of the New Channel 10 July 1849, by J. H. Burgess (Ulster Museum).

alternative accommodation at Queen's Quay across the river.

The construction of Donegall Quay brought to a virtual close the once flourishing but now restricted shipyards which had been developed near the dry docks. The first of these had been set up in 1795 by William Richie, who had arrived four years before from Saltcoats in Ayr accompanied by his brother Hugh, probably at the invitation of the Board. A few years later, in 1798, Hugh Richie set up a yard of his own. Both yards prospered and by 1811 William Richie's concern had built thirty-two ships of up to 450 tons burden. Several of these were of Irish oak, but imported timber had to be used for most of the vessels as virtually all accessible native timber had been cut down by the beginning of the eighteenth century. On his retirement in the 1820s, Richie's yard was taken over by his assistant Charles Connell, who takes the credit for the launching of the

William Ritchie's shipbuilding yard, Belfast, about 1810, artist unknown (Ulster Museum).

'Aurora', of 700 tons, in 1839, the first passenger steamship built in Ireland; whilst Hugh Ritchie's yard, in the course of time, passed into the ownership of another Scot, Alexander McLaine.

Within a generation these men put Belfast at the forefront of Irish shipbuilding; providing over 200 jobs in the yards with many more in the engineering, cordage and canvas manufactories. A new Harbour Office, to replace the old Office on the quay near Victoria Square, was built on the site of William Ritchie's yard in 1854: McLaine's yard, just north of the dry docks, had its access to the river curtailed, whilst the adjacent firm of Thompsons and Kirwan were provided with a new yard on Queen's Island, where the Board, determined to reserve the Antrim side of the new channel for commercial docks, had already provided a large timber pond and a 1,000 ton capacity patent slip to encourage the Island's development as a shipbuilding centre.

Clarendon Dock and Harbour Office, 1859 by A. C. Stannus (Belfast Harbour Commissioners). The Harbour Office, opened in 1854, was designed by the harbour engineer, George Smith, and occupies the site of William Ritchie's shipyard.

Despite the attraction of virtually unlimited space and proximity to deep water, the facilities offered at the Island were not at first fully appreciated. The twelve hour working day meant that, for much of the year, the workforce had to make the ferry crossing in the dark and all materials had to be brought in by water. However in 1853, Robert Hickson, seeking an outlet for the products of his new ironworks at Eliza Street, set up a successful iron shipbuilding yard beside the patent slip. Though Hickson's knowledge of shipbuilding was slight, the yard flourished under the capable direction of his manager, Edward Harland, who, in 1858, bought the yard for £5,000 with the help of a loan from a close family friend, G. C. Schwabe, a Liverpool merchant, whose nephew was Harland's personal assistant, Gustav Wolff. Wolff became a partner and in 1861 the firm became known as Harland and Wolff, owing much of its early success to Schwabe's help in obtaining orders from the Bibby Line, of which he was a principal shareholder. It was an opportune time for their

Belfast from the River Lagan about 1864 (Ulster Museum).

venture. The stranding of the 'Great Britain' in Dundrum Bay for a year in 1846 had proved the strength of iron construction; world trade was expanding rapidly, and new and larger ships were urgently needed. Harland's gradually expanded their facilities—absorbing, in 1859, the small wooden shipbuilding yard set up by Thompsons and Kirwan in 1851—until by 1870 they had six slips and a labour force of 2,400, providing badly needed employment for Belfast men to complement that available to women in the vast textile mills.

These decades saw many changes, and the opening of the Victoria Channel in 1849, together with the development of the railways, and the advent of cheap steam-powered sea transport did much to encourage trade. So much so that, though Belfast's port facilities had

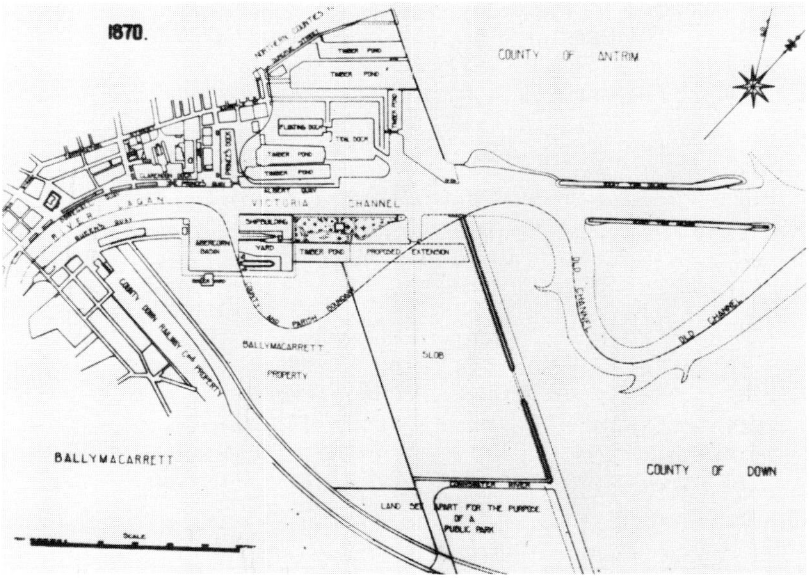

Plan of Belfast harbour in 1870 (Belfast Harbour Commissioners).

been modernised less than twenty years previously, by the 1860s they had become inadequate once again and in 1863 work was started on extensive new docks on both the Antrim and Down sides of the new channel.

Had Captain McKibben, the harbour master in 1837, paid a return visit in 1870 he would scarcely have recognised his surroundings. From the new Harbour Office he would have observed a great change in the number and type of vessels thronging the quays; since

BANQUET

TO

His Excellency the Lord-Lieutenant,

Harbour Office, 2nd October, 1867.

LIST OF TOASTS.

1.—"THE QUEEN," . . . . . . *The Chairman.*

2.—"THE PRINCE OF WALES, THE PRINCESS OF WALES, AND REST OF THE ROYAL FAMILY," *The Chairman.*

3.—"THE LORD-LIEUTENANT," . . *The Chairman.*

4.—"THE ARMY AND NAVY," . . *The Chairman.*
Lord de Ros. | *Admiral Seymour.*

5.—"THE HOUSES OF PARLIAMENT," *The Chairman.*
Lord Downshire. | *Sir Thomas Bateson, Bart.*

6.— *Lord-Lieutenant.*

7.—"LORD DONEGALL, LORD OF THE CASTLE," . . . . *The Chairman.*
Mr. Torrens.

8.—"THE MAYOR AND CORPORATION OF BELFAST," . . . . . *Edward O'Neill, M.P.*
The Mayor.

9.—"THE BOROUGH MEMBERS," . *The Chairman.*
Mr. Lanyon.

10.—"THE TOWN AND TRADE OF BELFAST," . . . . . . *Lord Mayor of Dublin.*
The President of the Chamber of Commerce.

11.—"THE LINEN TRADE OF ULSTER," *Lord Templetown.*
Mr. W. Ewart, jun.

12.—"THE BANKING INTERESTS OF BELFAST," . . . . . . *Mr. C. M'Garel.*
Mr. J. Thomson.

13.—"THE SHIP-BUILDING TRADE," *The Chairman.*
Mr. M'Laine and Mr. Harland.

14.—"ENGINEERS," . . . . *The Chairman.*
Mr. W. H. Lizars.

15.—"CONTRACTORS," . . . . . *The Chairman.*
Mr. Thomas Monk. | *Mr. Hick.*

Banquet in honour of the marquis of Abercorn on the occasion of the opening of the Abercorn Basin, 1867 (Belfast Harbour Commissioners). No fewer than 15 toasts were honoured.

the 1830s traffic had increased fourfold, and more than half the ships were now either screw or paddle steamers. Where formerly there had been only sand and mud banks there were now busy docks and engineering works. Across the river he would have seen the new Abercorn Basin, which had been opened by the marquis of Abercorn in October 1867, and occupied part of the old river bed. To the south was the Queen's Quay, where most of the half-million tons of coal brought in each year by the sailing colliers was discharged. The most imposing sight, however, was to be had in the noisy shipyard of Harland and Wolff, where, rising high on the nearest slipway was the mighty hull of the 'Oceanic', the first of many famous liners to be built by the company for the White Star Line. Downstream on the Antrim side, work was in progress on the new Spencer Dock, where such quays as had been completed were already pressed into service.

The vast amount of spoil from the new works, and from the deepening of the waterways, was used to reclaim yet more land to meet the anticipated expansion of the commercial and shipbuilding areas. Belfast's industrial capacity was given a great boost when, in 1880, Harland's set up works to provide engines for their ships, and two years later such was the demand that they extended the yards to occupy the northern end of Queen's Island, which for thirty years the Board had allowed the public to use as a pleasure ground, and

The 'Oceanic' passing the Musgrave Channel works near the East Twin in 1899 (Belfast Harbour Commissioners).

which, with its large 'Crystal Palace' as a focal point, had been the site of many fetes and amusements.

By now other shipbuilding firms were being established in the port, and shipbuilding output, some 20,000 gross tons in 1881, rose to over 80,000 tons by the end of the decade, as Workman, Clark and Co., and MacIlwaine and McColl added their output to that of Harland and Wolff. The successful launching of the new firms in the face of established competition is remarkable, and while it was due in part to increasing demand, an examination of the lists of the shipowners who placed the early orders shows the continued importance of the role played by family connections. Thereafter bold technical innovation, sound workmanship and personal integrity ensured that, once made, the connections were seldom broken and 'Belfast built' became synonymous with the best in ship construction. In 1893 Workman and Clark took over MacIlwaine and MacColl's yard and rivalled Harland and Wolff in size, both firms on occasion heading the tonnage returns of the world's shipbuilders.

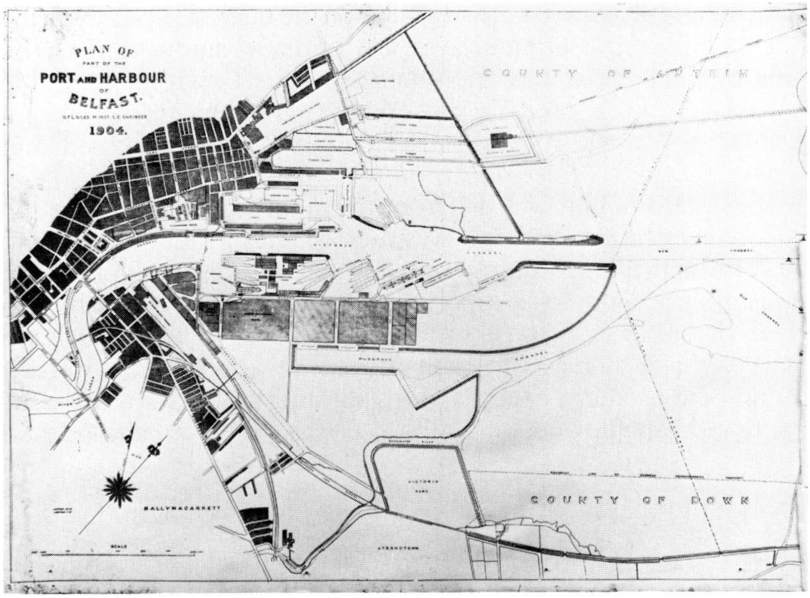

Plan of Belfast harbour in 1904 (Belfast Harbour Commissioners).

By 1894 all the available land bordering the Victoria Channel had been put to use for docks or shipbuilding. The Alexandra Graving Dock had been opened in 1889 to accommodate the long, lean ships that Harland had pioneered, and the York Dock was well under way. Additional land for docks and shipbuilding was required. Where was it to be provided? In spite of the general policy of commerce on the Antrim side and shipbuilding on the Down side, areas of slobland on both sides were proposed for development. The Antrim side had the advantage that docks there would be nearer the commercial heart of the city, whilst, on the other hand, on the Down side the old river course offered a ready-made start to a new channel. After some controversy the Down scheme won the day. The Musgrave Channel was started in 1899 and completed four years later, yielding 140 acres of reclaimed ground.

The steady expansion of trade continued during the first decade of the twentieth century. In 1912 the city's trade exceeded 3,000,000 tons and the produce of her shipyards was just under 200,000 gross tons, helped by the completion of the ill-fated 'Titanic', and its sister ship the 'Olympic', both constructed under the 'Great Gantry', and

The 'Titanic' under the Great Gantry, Queen's Island, 1911 (Ulster Transport Museum). The Great Gantry was built specially for the construction of the Titanic and her White Star Line sister ships.

which, when built, could just be accommodated in the new Thompson Graving Dock opened in 1911, at that time the largest dry-dock in the world.

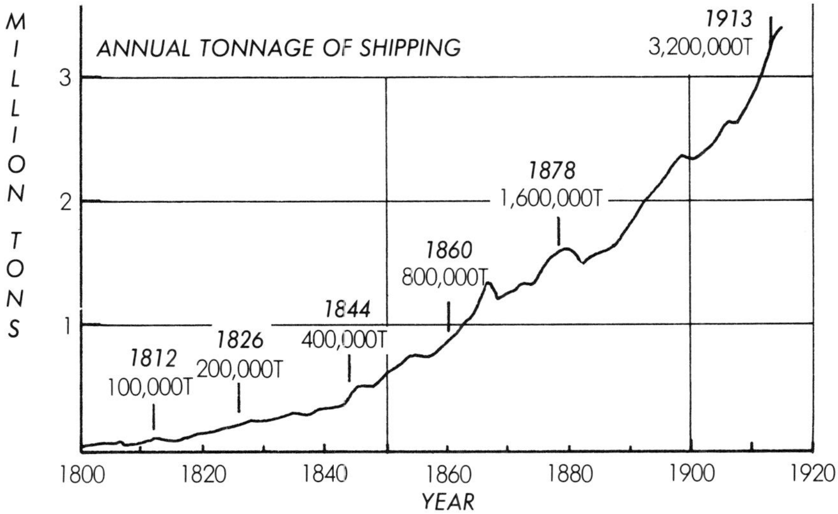

Graph 1 Annual tonnage of shipping cleared at Belfast between 1800–1914.

The tonnage of shipping at Belfast, 50,000 tons in 1800, doubled and redoubled every 15 years, reaching 1,600,000 tons by 1878 and doubling again to 3,200,000 tons by 1913.

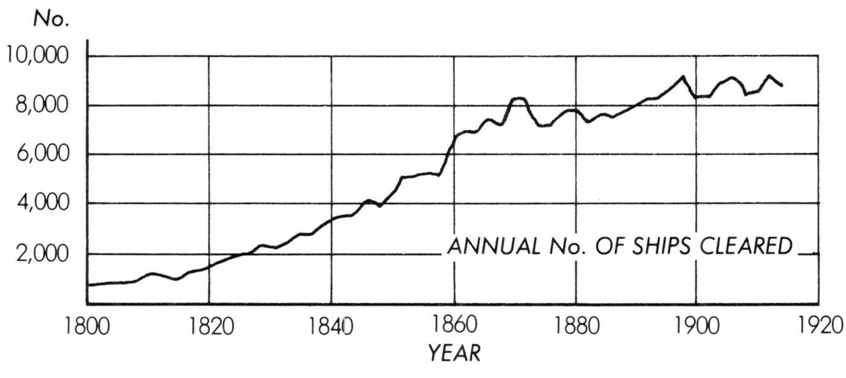

Graph 2 Annual number of ships cleared at Belfast between 1800–1914.

The annual number of vessels trading to Belfast, just under 800 in 1800, rose steadily to nearly 7,000 by 1860. From then until 1914, despite a fourfold increase in trade, the number of ships employed only increased by some 30 per cent as first iron then steel ships of rapidly increasing capacity came into general use.

Belfast had become the largest port in Ireland and led the world as a centre of shipbuilding. Every aspect of city life was influenced by its success. Its sprawling docks and yards gave direct employment to thousands and indirectly to many more in the engineering firms which provided specialist support and supplies. The local ownership of over 200 ships, totalling more than 300,000 tons, brought steady work for the ship repairers, chandlers and agents. Behind these was the essential support provided by the local banks and commercial houses. The decision of the Irish house of commons in 1785 to give responsibility for the port's development to those whose prosperity depended on its success could hardly have had a more comprehensive vindication.

5.'The Northern Athens' and after

John Hewitt

By 1800 Belfast was a seaport and market town of about 20,000 inhabitants. It had a theatre, several newspapers, a White Linen Hall, with a library founded by a Society for Promoting Knowledge, Exchange and Assembly rooms, a Literary Society (for men only), and a busy little group of educated people, mainly clergymen, doctors, schoolmasters, and so it became affectionately considered by them to be 'the Northern Athens'. Even so late as 1826 a poem was published with that title, though perhaps with an ironic intent.

To meet the demand of an informed readership, printers were eager to produce local editions of books popular across the water—Burns' poems had a dozen or so Belfast reprints—and to publish little books of verse, if their authors could persuade well-wishers to order copies before printing. One of these, *Juvenile Poems* (1806), by Thomas Romney Robinson (1793–1868), the twelve year old son of an itinerant English painter, had an edition of which over 2,000 copies were pledged—the profit took him to Trinity College, Dublin. Only a few lines of it now have any interest, those addressed to William Ritchie, who had been invited to start shipbuilding in the town:

> Ingenious Ritchie! Commerce now may smile
> And shed her blessings o'er Hibernia's Isle,
> Go, teach her sons to raise the ships on high
> The pointed masts, high towering to the sky . . .

Far more stimulating was little Dr William Drennan (1754–1820). Retiring from his practice in Dublin to Cabin Hill, he used his leisure well, starting a monthly magazine, helping to establish the Academical Institution, lending a hand to all the progressive causes. So he fairly described himself as:

> Of taste more than talent, not learned tho' of letters,
> His creed without claws and his faith without fetters.

The poem from which these lines come, with other witty verses, satires and translations from the French, Greek and Latin, was printed in *Fugitive Verses* (1815), which also has an address to the actress Mrs Siddons, who had played in Belfast twice.

A friend of Drennan's, the Rev. Dr William Hamilton Drummond (1778–1865), minister of the second congregation in Rosemary

The Cabin on the hill, residence of Dr William Drennan (*The Junior Campbellian, 1941*).

Street, ran a boy's boarding school, and gave public lectures on scientific subjects. Robinson was one of his hearers. Besides all this he took time to write a long, topical *Battle of Trafalgar* (1806), and the longer *Giant's Causeway* (1807), with a formidable array of prose notes on the geology, legends and history of the Antrim coast.

Drummond had come from Larne; another versewriter, Mary Balfour (c. 1780–1819) was the daughter of a deceased Limavady rector. She started a school for young ladies near where the Bank Buildings now stand. Her *Hope, a Poetic Essay and Various other Poems* (1810) in its titlepiece deals with consumption, then a deadly scourge. One pathetic couplet still sticks in my memory:

> The child of genius more securely thine
> Keeps to his vigil at thy fatal shrine

A melodrama by her, *Kathleen O'Neill*, was played at the theatre in 1814. Later she left for Larne and its healthy sea breezes, but died there shortly.

Another outsider, James Stuart (1764–1840), came from Newry to edit the *Belfast Guardian*. His *Poems on Various Subjects* (1811) use not only the fashionable couplet, but blank verse, and complicated lyrical stanzas. With these he exhibited the keenest eye and ear for natural phenomena among our local poets:

> From the low marsh the snipe delighted springs
> And the glad mallard claps his dappled wings

These five, and scores of our other verse writers followed the literary modes and conventions of the English eighteenth century, the Augustan age; so we may fairly think of them as colonial, though Drennan was edging away to something specifically Irish. Even in these days London was culturally influential, and an economic magnet for ambitious writers; and just at this time a Dr John Stewart from Belfast was winning some reputation there for his *Pleasures of Love* (1805) and succeeding volumes, all now forgotten.

But this colonial relationship was about to change as the north of Ireland was grappled to south-west Scotland and north-west England in the drive of the Industrial Revolution, which, with its spinning mills, factories and foundries, broke up the old cottage crafts. The town quadrupled its population in fifty years, drawing workers and their families from the surrounding countryside. In these years too, evangelical and fundamentalist religion rapidly gained ground among the new workers and their industrial masters to such an extent that the more liberal and tolerant section of the presbyterians was driven out. The leader in this change was Henry Cooke, a remarkable orator and an astute politician. He also exerted his influence to tie the evangelicals to the landowners of the tory party. Identifying catholicism with nationalism, he became an intrepid opponent of Daniel O'Connell in his struggle for emancipation and home rule. The new industrialists shared his ideology and the increasing labouring classes succumbed to sectarianism and outbursts of rioting.

Intelligent young men in the professions, and a few among the mercantile and industrial groups were turning to the natural sciences as less controversial than the arts. The Belfast Natural History and Philosophical Society (BNH & PS) was founded in 1821, and the Museum was opened ten years later. In obedience to

Samuel Ferguson (1810–86), by F. W. Burton.

Cooke's views theatre became rather suspect, attractive only to dissolute labourers, without dignity and moral responsibility. But before we leave the pre-Victorian decades we should note that the year 1810 marks the birth in Belfast of Samuel Ferguson, the most nationally important poet to have been born here. The Fergusons were landowners in SE Antrim, but Samuel's father dissipated his share of the estate and Samuel, the youngest son, was born in his mother's parent's house in High Street; his grandfather being a clockmaker and amateur astronomer. Educated at the Academical Institution, the lad became keenly interested in the Irish language, and formed a private study class with his friends Thomas O'Hagan (later lord chancellor) and George Fox, who lived with his widowed mother in North Street. In 1832 Ferguson wrote his at once popular 'The Forging of the Anchor', the subject of which he must have encountered among the local workshops. When he later published his translations from the Irish, his version of 'The County of Mayo', he always ascribed to Fox, who had a helping hand in its making. Though Sir Samuel, as he later became, never forgot his northern origins, his distinguished career in scholarship and literature ran its course in the institutions and society of viceregal Dublin.

The poets publicly recognised in the queen's reign were very different from the sophisticated Augustans who had gone before. A completely representative figure was William McComb (1793–1873). headmaster of the Brown Street school, he became a stationer and publisher in Cornmarket, where he produced Cooke's propagandist journal. With a busy life of committees assidously serving his master's interests, he brought out half a dozen books of verse culminating in his *Poetical Works*(1864). Saluted as 'The Laureate of Presbyterianism' in his heyday, his verses are dull, and can now only be read with effort. One of the books he sponsored was Tom Gilmore's *Norah O'Connor The Factory Girl* (1859). This was the first sizeable poem to come from local industry. Cast in a variety of verse forms, it has some pathos, but a great deal of sentimentality and no verbal distinction:

> Manufacturing City! The din and the smoke
> That ever are with thee thy fortune have made . . .

More interesting than either of these, or than the lugubrious Canon William McIlwaine (1807–85) of St George's, who composed the 'Ode for the Inauguration of the Ulster Hall Organ' in 1862, was Francis Davis (1810–85). An orphan, he came from Hillsborough to learn the craft of muslin-weaving. While following this in Glasgow and Manchester, before coming back about 1840, he had taught himself French and Latin, and had gained notice for his ballads in *The Nation.* There, because of the fame of that other Davis, Thomas, the Young Ireland leader, he was persuaded to append 'The Belfastman' to his signature. His first book *Lispings of the Lagan* (1849) was followed by *Miscellaneous Poems* (1852).

In 1855 a subscription was raised to put up a statue to Frederick Richard Chichester (1826–52), the young earl of Belfast who had died, like Keats, in Italy. Genuinely esteemed for his benefactions, among other things he had written songs to be sold for Famine relief and had given a series of lectures, afterwards published as *Poets and Poetry of the XIXth Century* (1852) in the Music Hall, May Street, to raise funds for the library of the Working Classes Association. He even wrote a novel in a few weeks. For the unveiling by the lord lieutenant, an ode was commissioned from the Dublin poet Denis Florence McCarthy. Stung by this, Davis brought out his own poem, *Belfast the City and the Man,* a much superior work.

This, the first free-standing statue in the town, sat in front of the Academical Institution, and soon became known as 'The Black Man'. However the temper of the town was changing. In 1859 we had the great revivals of 'The Year of Grace', when, among other events, 20,000 assembled in the Botanic Gardens to fall into a state of emotional hysteria and agonise, and seek salvation. And when the champion of evangelical orthodoxy died and a statue to the Rev. Henry Cooke was proposed, it seemed appropriate to the dominant mood that it should be erected on the site where the young earl's stood. So, in 1876, Cooke, the new 'Black Man', was set up, with his back turned to the institution which had been his bugbear. After some wandering the earl's statue found a resting place in the City Hall.

As a friend of William Thompson, the great naturalist, Davis was once invited to see an Egyptian mummy unwrapped in the Museum. Years later, in his book *The Tablet of Shadows* (1861) he included a long poem entitled 'Kabooti'. (She has been given a new name in the Ulster Museum, but, for my generation, she will always be Kabooti, and looking at her, we will think of Davis and Thompson who saw her unwrapped.) Davis' best and biggest book, *Earlier and Later Leaves, or an Autumn Gathering* (1878) is often referred to as his collected poems, but it does not include 'The City and The Man', 'Kabooti', or the sequence he wrote in memory of the prince consort, which earned him a medal from the queen and a public dinner in Belfast.

Criticised for his radical and nationalist verses, and never wholly or consistently accepted, Davis led a hand-to-mouth existence, and just before his death turned catholic. Had he lived in a more sympathetic atmosphere, in some literary circle, he might have achieved some degree of excellence, but the cultural tone of the town was now unashamedly philistine. The town council, sharing that tone, delayed for decades implementing legislation to provide a public library. Such a pursuit as writing poetry was not thought proper for a respectable citizen to admit, a frivilous, unmanly hobby, with no promise of financial gain. So while the streets had their crop of anonymous ballads like 'The Boys of Sandy Row' or 'The Battle of the Navvies', the only prominent people who dared to admit their folly were the journalists of the ephemeral papers, like Robert A. Wilson (c. 1820–75) better known as 'Barney Maglone', a bohemian apparition in a vast cloak, or Hugh Hankin (1793–1853) and Andrew James McKenna (1837–73), both buried at Friar's Bush, where, surprisingly, McKenna has his bust.

Among more decorous and responsible citizens one or two defaulters stirred. Robert Patterson (1802–72), mill furnisher, town councillor, naturalist, one of the founders of the BNH & PS, had a little book of his verse privately printed by the family after his death, and Dr John Swanwick Drennan (1809–93) had his elegant verses posthumously printed in *Poems and Sonnets* (1895). (Half a century before he had been happy enough to have some of his work included to fill out a reprint of his father's.) An intelligent and stylish rhymer, one of our very best, it is odd to read among his sonnets one against home rule. Clearly with the tides of time this liberal unionist, as he called himself, no longer shared his father's republican faith. Another member of the cresting middle class, Joseph John Murphy (1827–94), of a mill-owning family, whose philosophic prose won him regard in metropolitan intellectual circles, published his *Sonnets and Other Poems* in 1890, when such an admission could do him little harm. You will find his work included in Miles' compendious anthology *Poetry of the Century.* With a fine intelligence and a benevolent nature, Murphy must certainly have been one of the best men to climb the steps of the Linen Hall Library.

Circumstances were already changing. Perhaps Murphy's book was a hint. In the public career of Samuel K. Cowan (1850–1915), poetry was no longer a hobby but a way of life. Born at Dunmurry, graduate of TCD, a major in the militia, his books run from *Poems* (1872) to *From Ulster's Hills* (1913), a span of over forty years, and if we add 'the fine art verses for twelve London publishers to the extent of 500 annually, the fifty booklets for Birthday, Christmas and other gifts', the two hundred songs set to music, and the many popular pieces in collections like Gary's *Elocutionist,* or Nesbit's *Unique Reciter,* we should have some idea of his industry and the range of his audience. He lived in no ivory tower; in his last book there were poems on the loss of the Titanic, the tragic fate of Captain Scott, the opening of the City Hall, and the second Home Rule Bill—all matters of wide popular interest.

In 1896 Cowan joined with five younger poets, forming a small literary club, the Kitkat Club, which published the appropriately titled *Sung by Six.* The best of these was James H. Cousins (1873–1956), for a time secretary to Sir Daniel Dixon, the lord mayor. Just then there was a great upsurge of interest in the Irish language, attracting young people of all denominations. Cousins, a methodist, joined the Gaelic League, and was introduced to the modern poetry of Yeats by Mrs M. T. Pender, the novelist mother of

The Shan Van Vocht

Yes Ireland shall be free
From the centre to the sea,
And hurrah for Liberty
Says the Shan Van Vocht.

VOL. I.—NO. 2. BELFAST, 7TH FEBRUARY, 1896. PRICE TWOPENCE.

Titlepiece of *The Shan Van Vocht,* February, 1896.

one of his fellow bards. Cousins realised that Dublin had suddenly become an active, creative place, the pulsing centre of the new Anglo-Irish literary movement. So in 1897 he left home for the capital, and thus began a lifelong journey which took him to India, where he had a useful career; a good man if not a great poet.

One of his fellow students at the Irish class was a young woman from Fermanagh, Alice Milligan (1866–1953). Educated at the Methodist College and in London, she settled in Belfast with her friend Anne Johnstone, and started a little republican monthly called *The Shan Van Vocht* (1896–99). They both wrote poems for this and for other journals, using pen names. Anne's, under the name of Ethna Carbery, became exceedingly popular in Ireland and in the United States, and were collected in *The Four Winds of Eirinn* (1902) just after her untimely death. Alice, like Cousins, went to Dublin to involve herself in the literary stir, and her poems came out there in *Hero Lays* (1908).

Theatre had been plugging along at its base in Arthur Square, with stock companies welcoming visits of well known players. In 1895 however, the Grand Opera House was built to provide a stage to suit the touring companies led by the great actor-managers of late Victorian and Edwardian days. But, unlike Dublin, there was nowhere to put on plays by Irish authors, using local actors.

In the autumn of 1902 two young Belfastmen travelled down to see for themselves what was afoot. There they saw Alice Milligan's *The Last Feast of the Fianna* and Cousin's *The Racing Lug.* Back home, they decided with their friends to form an Ulster branch of the Irish Literary Theatre, and to act in their own plays. Before the end of the year they had managed to stage Yeats' *Kathleen Ni Houlihan,* written that very year, and *The Racing Lug,* in St Mary's minor hall. A poster for this attracted the attention of Joseph Campbell (1879–1944), and drew him into the group. By 1904 they had produced *The Reformers* by Lewis Purcell (David Parkhill), and *Brian of Banba* by

Joseph Campbell, by Estella Solomons (Ulster Museum).

Bulmer Hobson, the two young men who had made that trip to Dublin, and so Ulster drama began with local plays and local voices. Over the next two years plays by Campbell, Parkhill and Rutherford Mayne (Sam Waddell) were added to the list, and by 1908 *The Drone*, by the far the best of these, established the kitchen comedy as the staple form.

The group also started a short-lived quarterly, *Uladh* (1905–6). Campbell wrote verses for Herbert Hughes' folk songs of Donegal (1904), and with his book *The Rushlight* (1906), found himself saluted as 'unquestionably among the finest of the younger Irish poets'. That same year, not being able to find employment, he left and never came back.

When Patric Gregory joined the poets he dedicated his *Ulster Folk* (1912) to 'my friends Lewis Purcell and Rutherford Mayne'; this consisted of a couple of dozen poems built up from odd fragments he had collected. It had been preceded by *The Lane of the Thrushes*

Decoration by John Campbell (Uladh, February 1905).

(1905) by Cathal O'Byrne and Cahir Healy, the cover of which was designed by Campbell's brother, John Campbell (1877–1957), who was to bring out a fuller collection of this verse in *The Grey Feet of the Wind* (1917), and to become a popular entertainer in song and story before he left for America.

This busy writing was not confined to those connected to the theatre, nor to men. *The Secret Hill* (1913), by Ruth and Celia Duffin of the Drennan clan, and Helen Lanyon with her booklets *The Hill O'Dreams* (1913) and *Fairy-Led* (1915), illustrated by another Duffin sister, gave women a voice, but the most massive of such works was Mrs Mary A. Hutton's blank verse translation of *The Tain* (1907), which ran to over 400 pages.

All this original verse was filled with fairies, tramps of both sexes, tinkers, turfcutters, mothers crooning cradle-songs in cabins in misty glens or by lonely shores. This was now the accepted fashion; it had had its tentative beginning in Ferguson's 'Fairy Thorn' sixty years before, and had been developed into the Myth of the Peasant Irishry by Yeats and Lady Gregory.

So from these voluble city dwellers there was not a word about where they lived and the people they lived among, until in 1917 Richard Rowley (1877–1947) brought out his *City of Refuge* and *City Songs* (1918), in which he wrote of the islandman, the stitcher, the clerk, and had mills and gantries in his verse, giving Belfast its first industrial poetry since Gilmore's *Norah O'Connor* of sixty years before. The modish peasant-cottage convention did not pass without a mocking voice on the stage in *The Mist That Does be on the Bog* (1909) and *Thompson in Tír Na n-Óg* (1912) by Gerald McNamara, one of the Morrow brothers who were the backbone of the Ulster Literary Theatre.

With the writing of fiction the story is very different. This came late to the island and later still to the north. Indeed John Gamble of Strabane (c. 1770–1831) was probably the earliest worth notice. Certainly the *Belfast Monthly Magazine* (1808–15) carried only sketches and short tales. There was also the circumstance that novels by their comparative bulk needed publishers and printers with considerably greater resources than were available locally, and that their authors usually preferred to be closer to the potentiality of wide readership, well stocked bookshops and the circulating libraries. So they tended to settle where these existed. Hence we can hardly claim Rosa Mulholland, later Lady Gilbert (1841–1921) as ours, for, though born here, she wrote her books in London and Dublin, and of her forty novels, with such titles as *Hester's Holiday* or *The Girls of Banshee Castle*, not one of her 'sweet and innocuous' stories was set here. F. Frankfort Moore was another to whom our claim is weak. In spite of his seventeen years on the *Belfast News Letter* staff, of his voluminous output only *The Ulsterman* (1914) had a contemporary northern setting. Of the better remembered,

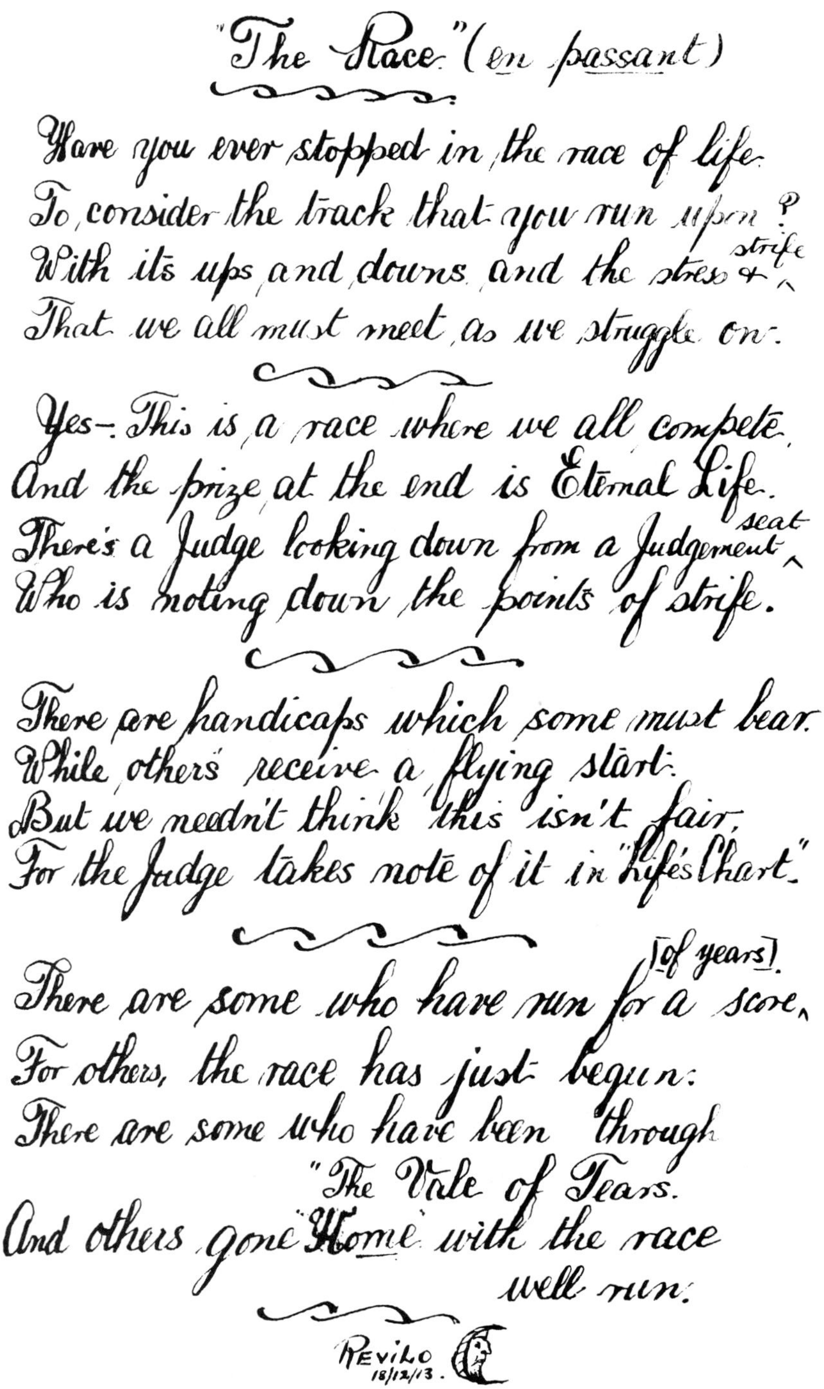
"The Race" (en passant)

Have you ever stopped in the race of life
To consider the track that you run upon?
With its ups and downs and the stress & strife
That we all must meet as we struggle on.

Yes – This is a race where we all compete,
And the prize at the end is Eternal Life.
There's a Judge looking down from a Judgement seat
Who is noting down the points of strife.

There are handicaps which some must bear.
While others receive a flying start.
But we needn't think this isn't fair,
For the Judge takes note of it in "Life's Chart".

There are some who have run for a score [of years],
For others, the race has just begun:
There are some who have been through
"The Vale of Tears.
And others gone "Home" with the race
well run:

REVILO
18/12/13.

Longhand poem by one of the Duffin sisters, which appeared on the inside back flap of a copy of *The Secret Hill,* held in the Linenhall Library.

George A. Birmingham (1845–1950) began his novel writing in the west of Ireland, and St John Ervine (1883–1971) left his native town at the age of nineteen.

It is worth remarking that in the last decades of our period several novelists, some of them resident here, produced novels of some historical interest, such as Samuel R. Keightley's *The Pikemen* (1894), Mrs M. T. Pender's *Green Cockade* (1898), and John Herron Lepper's *A Tory in Arms* (1916). Even George Birmingham had his *Northern Iron* (1907). These and other novels of this kind usually drew their subjects from the Williamite Wars, the Siege of Derry, and the '98 Rebellion.

St John Ervine; playwright, novelist, biographer, by William Conor (Ulster Museum).

So for Belfast novels we are left with Archibald McElroy's *A Banker's Love Story* (1908), in which Belfast is Spindleborough and the Ulster Bank is the Union Bank; and an imaginative and surprising work, *The Unpardonable Sin* (1907) by James Douglas. Its period is the centenary of the Rebellion. Belfast is called Bigotsborough and the first half is a trenchant account of life here at the time, with vigorously presented displays of the pulpit politics of identifiable rabble-rousing clergymen. Thinly disguised, Maud Gonne and her poet-lover appear at a public demonstration; but the second half is more concerned with the rise of a charismatic evangelist into the stratosphere of fantasy. By the date of publication Douglas was safely launched on a highly successful Fleet Street career, to end as editor of the *Sunday Express*.

The only novelist of significant stature to live permanently among us was Forrest Reid (1875–1947). He first comes to our attention with *Uladh* and the Literary Theatre. We tend to think of him as the master of the subtler aspects of middle class boyhood and adolescence, but as John Wilson Foster has written:

> Certainly there are flashes of realism in *The Kingdom of Twilight* (1904), Reid's first novel, and *At the Door of the Gate* (1915) his sixth, especially when Reid wishes to portray the squalor of working-class Belfast. But

Forrest Reid; novelist, literary critic, autobiographer, by J. S. Sleator (Ulster Museum).

one could with more justification call Reid a gentle fantasist.

Though he was by far the city's greatest novelist, his deep but narrow sensitivities throw little light on our idiosyncratic tensions and eruptions, or on the surprising durability and resilience of our values.

6. Of art and artists

Eileen Black

Belfast in the late eighteenth century was a small town with few resident artists and little artistic activity. The first professional painter to settle in the community was an artist who earned his living primarily by portraiture, Joseph Wilson. He arrived around 1770, possibly attracted by the market he saw amongst the town's increasingly prosperous merchant class. Although Wilson painted both portraits and landscapes, it was the former which were in demand in Belfast at this time. There was to be little demand for landscape painting in the north for another fifty years.

Nothing is known of Wilson's origins and training and regrettably little about his life as a whole. During the 1770s and 1780s, he worked in Belfast and Dublin, building up extensive practices in both places. His sitters were almost all from the professional and merchant classes. He also painted a number of Volunteer portraits and may in fact have been a Volunteer himself. Benn's *History of Belfast* (p. 755) records a Joseph Wilson as being a member of the 3rd Division of the Belfast 1st Volunteer Company. A Joseph Wilson is also recorded as belonging to Orange Lodge of Belfast 257 (in

Joseph Wilson *Lieutenant Hyndman,* oil on canvas 77 × 64 cms (Ulster Museum). The lieutenant, an officer in the Belfast 3rd Volunteer Company, may have met Wilson through the Volunteers, or perhaps through Orange Lodge of Belfast 257.

spite of its name, a Masonic Lodge closely linked to the Volunteers), to which lieutenant Hyndman (Ill. 1) also belonged. It would not be too improbable to assume that these three Wilsons—artist, Volunteer, Mason—are the one person, filling out our scant knowledge of the painter with a brief insight into his involvement in local affairs.

As for his art, the majority of Wilson's portraits are somewhat crudely painted. His sitters often have a rather lifeless appearance and he seems to have understood little of the principles of perspective—note the odd looking columns in the background of the Hyndman portrait. His paintings, however, have a great deal of charm, and as local historical records, are invaluable. He died at Echlinville, Co. Down on 13 March 1793, being described in his death notice as 'a very worthy honest man'.

Wilson's place as foremost portrait painter was filled by an English artist, Thomas Robinson (fl. 1790–1810). Born in Windermere, Robinson studied for a time with the portrait painter George Romney before settling in Dublin about 1790. He moved north three years later, first to Laurencetown, Co. Down, then, in 1798, to Lisburn, where he painted what is probably his best-known piece, *The Battle of Ballynahinch* (now in the National Gallery of Ireland), depicting the last phase of the battle of 12 June 1798 between Crown troops and the United Irishmen. The painting was raffled in November 1798. Robinson obviously cast a shrewd eye on the market, painting such a political piece so shortly after the actual event.

In 1801, he moved to Belfast, where he acquired a wide and fashionable clientele. His most ambitious portrait *The Entry of Lord Hardwicke into Belfast as Lord Lieutenant, 27 August 1804* hangs in the Belfast Harbour Office. This extremely large painting ($5^1/_2$ ft x 8 ft) is of particular interest to local historians because of the number of local worthies which it contains. The artist hoped to sell the painting by raffle on 1 September 1807, but failed to raise sufficient money from his Belfast patrons. In a fit of pique, he altered the background (which originally showed Donegall Place), added a statue of Nelson, and exhibited the painting in Dublin in 1809, under the title *A Military Procession in Belfast in Honour of Lord Nelson.* (That the event never took place, and that there was never a statue of Nelson in Belfast, was obviously irrelevant to him.) Despite popular feeling for the hero of Trafalgar, however, the picture still failed to sell and was presented to the Harbour Commissioners in 1852 by the artist's son.

As an artist, Robinson was ambitious, with his large canvases of crowd scenes, and with his extensive use of symbols. Not for him the simple background of curtain or landscape. The portrait of his son (Ill. 2) ranks among his finest, with the figure well drawn, and mood and atmosphere created by a delicate use of light and shade. Though his portrait practice was extensive, Robinson seems to have had to struggle to survive—Martha McTier, whose letters to her brother Dr William Drennan provide us with a fascinating glimpse of Belfast at this time, visited the painter in 1807 and described him as 'an interesting, sensible man, of great simplicity and *very poor*'. The artist moved to Dublin in 1808, dying there two years later.

Thomas Robinson *Thomas Romney Robinson (1792–1882)*, oil on canvas 119.4 × 99.1 cms (Armagh County Museum). The portrait shows the artist's son strewing flowers on the grave of George Romney, Robinson's art teacher. The junior-sized lyre (symbol of the poet) in young Thomas's hand, alludes to his poetic talent, as author of *Juvenile Poems,* published in 1806 to great local acclaim.

The most prominent of Belfast's artists in the early decades of the nineteenth century were Thomas Clement Thompson, Hugh Frazer, Samuel Hawksett, Joseph Molloy and James Atkins. Although one can only speculate, there was doubtless a certain amount of competition between them, given the size of the community they served. These years saw a growing interest, on the part of the nobility and gentry, in the careers of Belfast's artists—the marchioness of Donegall sat to both Thompson and Hawksett, and patronised the publication of Proctor's *Belfast Scenery* (illustrated by Molloy), while Atkins was sent to Italy, and financially assisted by the marquis of Downshire, the marquis of Londonderry and Mrs Batt of Purdysburn. Such encouragement undoubtedly played an important part in the development of fine art in the town in these uncertain early years.

Thompson (c. 1778–1857), who was probably a native of Belfast, remains a shadowy figure. Trained in Dublin, he began his career as a miniaturist, but switched to large-scale oil portraiture about 1810. Although his portraits have been described as 'solid though uninspired',[2] he could on occasion produce work of high quality, as seen in (Ill. 3). He worked in both Belfast and Dublin for several years before settling in London in 1817. While we know little of his life or circumstances, one thing is certain—he was a hard-working individual, exhibiting about 150 paintings in London alone,

T. C. Thompson *John McCance MP (1772–1835)*, painted 1825, oil on canvas 130 × 101.5 cms (Ulster Museum). The artist's skill as a portraitist can be seen in this painting—the sitter's eyes seem almost alive and his mouth about to smile.

between 1816 and 1857, besides many more in Dublin. After moving he returned to Ireland only for occasional visits.

Hugh Frazer (fl. 1813–1861) was the first Ulster landscape artist of note. Landscape painting was slow to emerge in the British Isles, only making an appearance as an art form in England in the early seventeenth century. Irish landscape painting did not begin to develop until about a century later. In the north, the development was even slower, and although Wilson, Robinson and Thompson had occasionally painted landscapes, it was not until the first third of the nineteenth century that Ulster artists began to specialize in scenes of their native countryside; a phenomenon almost certainly related to the increasing wealth of Belfast's middle class, now seeking pretty views to decorate their living and drawing rooms.

Frazer, who was from Dromore, studied in Dublin and established a successful practice as a landscape painter in Dublin and Belfast. In 1837, he was elected a member of the Royal Hibernian Academy (RHA) and taught painting in the Academy school for several years. He is best known for his northern scenes (Ill. 4). He seems to have been highly articulate and greatly esteemed by his fellow artists, writing an *Essay on Painting* (published in 1825), and being elected to the presidency of the Belfast Association of Artists in 1836. Regrettably, details of his life remain something of a mystery and little is known of him after his resignation from the RHA in 1861.

The third of our five painters, Samuel Hawksett, generally recorded as having been born in 1776 and having died in 1851, was in fact born in 1801 (in Cookstown, Co. Tyrone) and died in 1859.[3] Nothing is known of his early life or training, but by 1825, he was

Hugh Frazer *View of Waringstown*, painted 1849, oil on canvas 63 × 76 cms (Ulster Museum). The standard of Frazer's work varies. His paintings, though topographically accurate and always interesting, are often marred by rather careless brushwork and poor draughtsmanship. This painting is arguably his best, with is uncharacteristic fine brushwork and close attention to detail.

exhibiting portraits at the RHA, and during the following two decades, became Belfast's leading portrait painter. In 1832, some of the members of the Board of the Academical Institution commissioned him to paint a portrait of William IV for the school. The Board's records (PRONI) show that the King gave Hawksett permission to copy his best portrait. Completed in 1836, the picture was to become an object of protracted dispute between the artist and the Institution. The Board was unwilling to accept Hawksett's bill of £100, because, as the records show, the commission had not come from them as a body, but from 'several Individuals in their private capacity'. It seems that Hawksett's account was to be paid by private subscription arranged by these individual Board members. Part of the sum was raised and given to the artist, but in spite of his continued pleading the matter of the money disappears from the Board's minutes. Ironically, the portrait seems also to have disappeared—possibly it was reclaimed by Hawksett. The incident is a reminder that life for pre-twentieth century artists, dependent for the most part on patronage (though some did eke out their earnings by giving art lessons), was often one of hardship and struggle.

As a portraitist, Hawksett is dull, if competent (Ill. 5). The value of his portraits lies more in their local historical worth than in their artistic merit. He seems to have lived in penurious circumstances—his trips to London to copy the king's portrait were made on borrowed money and his letters to the Institution's Board hint at embarassed finances. His life appears to have been a hard one, his

Samuel Hawksett *Robert Langtry*, oil on canvas 135.1 × 101.2 cms (Ulster Museum). The sitter seems lifeless and almost devoid of facial expression. The portrait, however, has an air of gravity befitting Langtry's position as a prosperous Belfast shipowner, who, incidentally, became the father-in-law of the famous Lily Langtry.

wife and daughter dying of cholera within a day of each other in 1849, and he ending his days in a lodging house in College Street.

Joseph Molloy (1798–1877) was born in Manchester but moved to Belfast with his family and studied at the Academical Institution. He taught art at Belfast Academy for two years before returning to the Institution in 1830 as drawing master, a post he held for forty years. Besides teaching art, he painted portraits and seascapes (Ill. 6), but is best known as the illustrator of E. K. Proctor's *Belfast Scenery* (1832), for which he provided thirty drawings of the seats of local gentry. His output was small, due to the fact that he spent most of his leisure hours (apart from during his early career) in literary rather than artistic activity. Writing in 1907, Robert Young, the Belfast architect, remembers him as 'an unassuming modest man and as different to the present day school of art trained teacher as one could imagine'.

The last of our group, James Atkins (1799–1833), the son of a house, sign and coach painter, entered the Academical Institution in 1817[4] and studied there for two years, winning a medal for oil portraiture in the drawing school examinations. So impressive was his talent that he was sent to Italy in 1819 to study the Old Masters, through the kindness of local benefactors. Regrettably, we know nothing of his life there. In December 1832, he left Rome and went to Constantinople to paint the sultan, before returning to Ireland, but developed consumption and died in Malta the following year. Fortunately for posterity, his paintings were shipped back to Belfast and auctioned in March 1835. He was highly gifted, as can be seen in

Joseph Molloy *Tilbury Fort, River Thames*, oil on canvas on board 30.5 × 40.6 cms (Ulster Museum). Molloy's talent was impressive, as evident in this seascape, with its realistic depiction of sky and sea.

(Ill. 7)—Belfast's artistic legacy was undoubtedly diminished by his early death.

By 1835, Belfast had expanded greatly, its population more than doubling since the turn of the century. The thriving community was now able to support a number of resident artists (the abovementioned and a few others of lesser importance), in consequence of the growing demand for portraits, miniatures and landscapes. As yet, however, there was no formal art society in the town, unlike

James Atkins *George Hamilton, Earl of Belfast, later 3rd Marquis of Donegall (1797–1883)*, painted 1824, oil on canvas 233.7 × 145.4 cms (Ulster Museum). This large portrait is a splendid achievement, especially considering that Atkins was a mere twenty-five years old when he painted it.

Dublin, where the Dublin Society had been encouraging the arts since 1739, by setting up a school and awarding prizes for painting and sculpture. Here the Society of Artists of Ireland (founded 1800) and the Royal Hibernian Academy (established 1823) provided continual support, and opportunity, by offering teaching facilities and mounting exhibitions.

Doubtless influenced by the example of the RHA, which had opened an Academy house in Abbey Street, Dublin, in 1826, the Belfast Association of Artists (BAA) was formed in 1836, with the object of holding annual exhibitions and raising funds for the erection of an Institute of Fine Arts in the town. The first office bearers were Hugh Frazer (president), Samuel Hawksett (treasurer) and Nicholas Crowley, a visiting artist, as secretary. The time was not ripe, however, and the venture collapsed in 1838, after three exhibitions had been held at the museum, College Square North. Nevertheless, despite its closure and the apparent lack of public interest in an Institute of Fine Arts, the BAA should not be considered a total failure. For the first time Belfast's artists were acting as a body, recognising the need for improvement in the arts in the north of Ireland, and attempting to do something about it. They were, however, over-optimistic as regards sponsorship. It was to be nearly another fifty years before an art society (the Belfast Ramblers' Sketching Club) became a permanent feature in Belfast's cultural life.

Elish Lamont *Miss O'Hara of Ballymena*, ivory miniature 10.8 × 8.2 cms (Ulster Museum). Although Elish's output was large, this is the only known miniature by her in a public collection. Her artistic gifts were limited. While the miniature shows her to have been skilled at painting drapery and fine detail, she seems to have been sadly lacking in the ability to make her sitter appear completely lifelike.

Besides Frazer, Hawksett and Atkins (posthumously), and several non-resident artists, two other noteworthy local artists exhibited with the BAA—Elish Lamont and Andrew Nicholl. Elish Lamont (1816–1870) or La Monte[5] as she preferred to be known (probably for business reasons) had a flourishing practice as a miniaturist in

Belfast from about 1838 to 1858 (Ill. 8), numbering many titled persons among her sitters. The daughter of John Lamont, a Belfast stationer, she had both artistic and literary ability and was something of a poet, publishing a book of ballads, *Christmas Rhymes* with her sister in 1846, and winning second prize in the Victoria Fete Poetry Competition of 1850, with *The Island Queen.* She has the distinction of being Belfast's earliest-known woman artist, and was to remain its sole professional female painter of note during her lifetime. Not until the end of the century, when careers for women became more acceptable, do we see the emergence of a number of professional women artists in Belfast.

Andrew Nicholl (1804–1886)—one of the most popular nineteenth-century artists with local buyers today—was born in Church Lane, the son of a bootmaker. After serving his time as an apprentice compositor with the *Northern Whig,* and giving drawing lessons in his leisure hours, he took up landscape painting on a full-time basis (Ill. 9), a bold step, but one in which he was helped and encouraged by his elder brother William, himself a competent painter. In 1830, by which time he had built up a substantial reputation, he left Belfast and thereafter lived variously in London, Belfast and Dublin, teaching landscape painting and sending works to the RHA (of which he became a member in 1860). He also spent a period in Ceylon, teaching drawing and painting in Colombo Academy.

During his early career, he undertook a good deal of book illustration, his work appearing in *Views of the Dublin and Kingstown Railway* (1834), *Fourteen Views in the County of Wicklow* (1835) and *Hall's Ireland* (1841–43). Shortly after his death (in London), almost 300 of his paintings were exhibited in Belfast, in order 'to vindicate the reputation of the late Mr Nicholl as an artist of no mean order'.

Andrew Nicholl *Belfast from Newtownbreda Churchyard,* watercolour on white paper 35.4 × 52.8 cms (Ulster Museum). This painting of Nicholl's, besides being finely and delicately executed, is a valuable record of Belfast and its environs in the mid 19th century.

Until 1849, Belfast lacked any kind of government-sponsored art school. On 6 December of that year, however, the Belfast Government School of Design opened its doors. The School, which was given accommodation in the Academical Institution, had as its main aim the cultivation of skilled and imaginative designers for the textile industry, by encouraging the development of artistic ability in artisans. By the opening date 130 artisans had enrolled and several ladies and gentlemen had applied to join the private classes.

The School based its hopes of success on the support of the linen industry (half its running costs were meant to come from private subscriptions), but this was not forthcoming, and it was forced to close in 1855. This undoubtedly had a detrimental effect on the locality's artistic life, as those desiring training were forced to study elsewhere. Belfast was to be without an official school of art for the next fifteen years.

James Glen Wilson *Emigrant Ship leaving Belfast,* painted 1852, oil on canvas 71.4 × 91.3 cms (Ulster Museum). This view of Belfast harbour was painted from the present Liverpool ferry berth at the Donegall Quay, just south of the entrance to the Clarendon Dock. The departing ship is being towed down the newly opened Victoria Channel, towards the open sea.

During its brief existence, several talented artists studied at the School of Design. Among these were Samuel McCloy, later to become Master of Waterford School of Art, Anthony Carey Stannus, President of Belfast Ramblers' Sketching Club 1885–1890, and James Glen Wilson, who attended probably as a private pupil, his father being a gentleman of independent means. Wilson's work in particular is of the highest quality, as can be seen from the *Emigrant Ship* (Ill. 10), a painting which is not only beautifully executed, but a useful historical record of Belfast harbour in the mid-nineteenth century, containing much valuable topographical detail.[6]

So far in this brief history, sculpture has not been mentioned, the

Patrick McDowell *Frederick Richard, Earl of Belfast (1827–1853),* executed 1855, bronze, height 209 cms (Belfast city council). This statue, Belfast's original 'Black Man' (so-called, presumably, because of its dark bronze colour) stood in College Square East until 1874, when it was moved to the old Town Hall in Victoria Street, to make way for the statue of Dr Henry Cooke (also known as the 'Black Man', despite its bronze having a green patina). The statue of Frederick Richard can be seen in Belfast City Hall.

reason being that until the early 1850s, the plastic arts played very little part in Belfast's artistic activities. On 1 November 1855, however, the town's first public statue, that of Frederick Richard, earl of Belfast (Ill. 11) was unveiled by the lord lieutenant in College Square East, in front of the Academical Institution. In erecting the statue, Belfast was following a trend which had been steadily growing in Britain since the 1820s, that of publicly commemorating individuals other than monarchs. It is also not too far-fetched to see in this effort at dignifying the town, Belfast's growing belief in itself as a centre of culture and commerce. Rather appropriately, the sculptor of the piece was the Belfast-born Patrick McDowell (1799–1870), who had lived in England since the age of twelve, and at the time of this commission was one of Britain's leading sculptors.

Belfast acquired two other public statues in the second half of the century—the prince consort on the Albert Memorial Clock (1869)—and the statue of Henry Cooke, which replaced that of the earl of Belfast in 1876. Both were by a sculptor with local connections, Samuel Ferres Lynn (1834–1876), a London-based former pupil of the School of Design and brother of the well-known local architect, W. H. Lynn. (Lynn, like several of the artists mentioned here, left Belfast to work elsewhere, probably finding the town's artistic life somewhat confining.) Sculpture, however, remained a minor part of the Belfast art scene at this time—only with the work of Rosamond Praeger towards the end of the century did it take on a greater local significance.

To return to painting, one of the major (though now somewhat forgotten) artists of the second half of the nineteenth century was Richard Hooke (1820–1908), a native of Co. Down who worked as a carpenter before taking up portrait painting. Though he moved to Manchester about 1860, the largely self-taught Hooke retained an extensive practice in Belfast, through annual visits to the town, Rodman's Gallery, in Donegall Place, hosting a number of well-publicised exhibitions of his work.

Though his portraits are rather dull (Ill. 12), Hooke seems to have been an interesting character, witty, articulate and well-read. While a majority of the artists referred to so far seem to have belonged to the middle class, Hooke, judging by his former trade of carpenter, appears to have had a skilled working class background. He became, in time, one of Manchester's most highly-respected citizens, the vice-president of the Manchester Literary Club (for which he wrote many papers 'generally distinguished by a peculiar vein of Hibernian humour'), and a Fellow of the Royal Astronomical Society. In addition, he served as a lieutenant in the 2nd Manchester Volunteers for twelve years. Appropriately for one whose clientele consisted mainly of Victorian industrialists and self-made men, many of his portraits are to be found in Belfast and Manchester City Halls, seats of civic dignity and pride.

Richard Hooke *George Benn (1801–1882),* oil on canvas 92.3 × 71.9 cms (Ulster Museum). Hooke's portraits tend to lack imagination and life, but record, like the camera (which he used), the essential details of the sitter. This portrait of the famous Belfast historian is competent but dull. Nevertheless, Hooke's portraits should not be too disparaged—although pedestrian, they are valuable records of Belfast society in the 19th century.

From 1855 (with the closure of the School of Design) until 1870, there was no official art school in Belfast. However, in that year, some leading citizens, deciding that the gap should be filled, set up a committee, the outcome of which was the establishment of a Government School of Art. This opened on 18 October 1870, once again in the Academical Institution. Aware of the fate of its predecessor, the headmaster in his inaugural address, made a particular appeal to the city's growing class of artisans:

> We especially invite the cunning artificer in brass and iron; we shall be disappointed if we do not meet the young mason, cabinet-maker, upholsterer, joiner, carver and gilder . . . in our classes; we have no hesitation in saying that we can impart instruction of practical value to the operative, no matter what the craft by which he earns his daily bread.

The School received wide support, and many donations towards its running costs. By the mid 1870s it was competing successfully with its British equivalents, with its pupils winning many prizes and awards in national examinations. Together with the publishing firm of Marcus Ward, which had a flourishing art department full of local talent, the School did much to advance the community's young artists.

Another encouraging sign was the advent of the Belfast Ramblers' Sketching Club in 1879. This provided a useful forum in which artists could meet, exchange ideas and hold exhibitions. It went from strength to strength, becoming the Belfast Art Society in 1890, and evolving, in 1950, into the Royal Ulster Academy of Arts. As such, it continues to flourish.

Of the many talented artists who frequented the club, perhaps one of the best-known was sculptor Rosamond Praeger (1867–1954) Born in Holywood, Co. Down, she was educated at Sullivan Upper

Rosamond Praeger *The Fairy Fountain,* marble 64.8 × 76.5 × 16.5 cms (Ulster Museum). Beautifully modelled, Praeger's figure of the little girl is represented with a skill which makes the marble almost seem to come alive.

Grammar School, Belfast, and after studying at the School of Art, went to the Slade School of Fine Art, London, in 1888, where she won a number of commendations. On completing her studies, she returned to Holywood, to live there for the rest of her life, sending works to exhibitions in Belfast, Dublin and London.

Early in her career, to help supplement her income (there being a smaller market generally for sculpture than for painting) she began to illustrate, and eventually write, children's books. Children, in fact, made up the bulk of her subject matter (Ill. 13). Her most famous piece, which brought her international acclaim, was a statue of a naked chubby little boy, *The Philosopher,* which can be seen in the Ulster Museum, Belfast. During her long career, she received many accolades, including the M.B.E., and had the distinction of becoming the first woman president of the Ulster Academy of Arts.

Another prominent member, now largely overlooked, was Sydney Mary Thompson (1847–1923). A member of the gentry (the family seat, Macedon, was a large imposing residence at Whitehouse), she began attending the School of Art in her middle twenties and won several prizes for design in the School's examinations. During the last two decades of the century, when women were playing an increasingly important role in the artistic life of the community, she established a reputation as one of Belfast's leading women artists (Ill. 14), being a frequent exhibitor with the Ramblers' Sketching Club and Belfast Art Society, of which she was honorary secretary for a time.

In 1910, she married a Swiss artist, Rodolphe Christen, and moved

Sydney Mary Thompson *By the Shore,* watercolour on white paper 22.8 × 31.5 cms (collection the author). Until recently, the artist's only known painting was an oil portrait in the Ulster Museum. In 1980, however, some of her works were unearthed in Scotland. From this painting, we can see that she was a fine landscape artist, capable of creating atmosphere and depth, and skilled in watercolour technique.

to Scotland. Thereafter, she seems to have ceased to paint. She did, however, keep in close contact with the Art Society, and became one of its official patrons in 1921. Although her paintings are now very scarce, there are doubtless many languishing unrecognised in local private collections.

Although his career extended beyond the nineteenth century, it seems fitting to end with the artist who could be called Belfast's own painter, he who more than any other has shown the essence of Belfast, its back streets and working class life—William Conor (1881–1968). Born on the Old Lodge Road, he studied at the School of Art, spent some time as an apprentice poster designer and then began to paint full-time. He became a familiar figure on the streets of Belfast, sketching the teeming life of the city: crowds of shipyard workers heading homewards, mill girls gossiping on street corners. His paintings can be found in many local collections, including that of the Ulster Folk and Transport Museum, where there is, quite properly, a Conor room. During both World Wars, he worked as an official war artist visiting munition works and army camps, recording Ulster's war effort. One of his drawings from the First World War (Ill. 15) is shown here. It seems a highly appropriate image with which to close this brief look at art in Belfast before 1914.

By the early years of the twentieth century, Belfast was paying increasing attention to the visual arts. The Belfast Free Public Library, Art Gallery and Museum, opened in 1890, was acquiring paintings, engravings and sculpture, under the expert guidance of a curator-in-

William Conor *Off, the Ulster Division,* executed 1915, charcoal and red chalk on paper 55 × 37.3 cms (Ulster Museum). These three cheerful young men of the 36th (Ulster) Division are heading off for the front, little aware of the horror and carnage before them.

charge. In 1901, Belfast corporation assumed responsibility for the flourishing Government School of Art, and after housing it temporarily in premises in North Street, established it as the Belfast School of Art, on the top floor of the magnificent new Municipal Technical Institute, opened in 1907. With this move, art was, as it were, given a permanent place in the community, for the old Government School of Art had had to operate in rented premises.

The previous century had seen severe setbacks in Belfast's burgeoning artistic life. The collapse of the town's first art society in 1838 and the closure of the School of Design had not augured well for the community's artistic development. However, the industrial expansion of the later decades of the nineteenth century assured the success of the Government School of Art, as not only art students but textile designers and craftsmen flocked to its classes. It could be said with some justification that the demands of industrialisation laid the foundation, and in large part set the direction of Belfast's artistic progress.

7. Popular entertainment

John Gray

The dramatic expansion of Belfast from country town to industrial city may, at first sight, suggest that little time was left for the pursuit of pleasure. However, though time and resources may have been limited the inhabitants of Belfast were as enthusiastic as any others in seeking entertainment; and what they chose to do reveals a good deal about social change during the period.

Public holidays provided the most general opportunity for leisure activity, and throughout the nineteenth century that most traditional of festivals—Easter, was celebrated with vigour. William Reed in his poem *Hill of Caves* published in 1818 has left us a graphic account of the celebration of Easter Monday in Belfast. As the title of the poem suggests the focal point for these 'sports' was high up on Cave Hill beneath the caves. It was no small occasion:

> Now group on group is seen to follow far,
> Like to a Persian army in array,
> On foot, on steed, coach, jingle cart and car—
> Towards the high hill of caves they wend their way.

Accompanied by the 'fiddle's flourish and the bag-pipe's grunting' the crowds ascended to an encampment on the plateau where 'tents had sprung up in every available patch of level or semi-level ground'. Here the revellers could dance to 'Hibernia's planxties' and 'Caledonia's reels', and 'quaff the cup of glee', or, as F. J. Bigger put it, rather more censoriously, engage in 'an excessive consumption of illicit spirits'. Food was plentiful and items ranging from cockles and mussels to yellow man could be bought by those who had not lost their all at endless games of chance. Then, at the close of the day, a blind harper, a suitable symbol for so traditional an assembly, serenaded the revellers on their descent to the town.

In succeeding years there were attempts to change the nature of the gathering. Politics intruded: in 1828 Orangemen from Carnmoney used the occasion for a demonstration, with the result that Dr Crolly, catholic bishop of Down and Connor, urged his parishioners to stay away; but much more significant were changes in social attitudes. Liberal presbyterianism was by then beginning to retreat before conservative orthodoxy, and accordingly the drinking, gambling, and courting associated with Cave Hill, and tolerated during the 1820s, were by the 1840s considered sinful.

This was made very clear by the anonymous author of *The Annals of Christ Church*, writing in 1844, who said that 'it was customary for multitudes to resort on Easter Monday to the Cave Hill, when with folly and riot the day was wasted, and scarcely an anniversary passed without loss of life.' The annals also make it clear that from 1834 the clergy connected with Christ church made strenuous efforts to organise alternative events, beginning 'the custom of collecting the schools together on this day and of giving them an annual feast with an excursion into the country', and in later years the managers of other schools made similar provision.

Allied to these efforts were those of the Tee Total Society, which in 1841 made a direct assault on the hill, and if we are to believe the *Northern Whig*, transformed the festivities of the day:

> Eloquent speeches in praise of sobriety and total abstinence from intoxicating drinks were delivered and frequently the caves were made to resound with the cheers of the multitude.

The contrast between the old ways and the new evangelical approach to Easter Monday is nowhere better expressed than in the account in *The Annals of Christ Church* of the excursion made in 1844:

> First came the Girls' division, each division consisting of twenty girls, preceded by their proper banner and under charge of one of the female teachers. There were twenty-three of these divisions. The Boys' divisions following were preceded by a beadle carrying the large white silk flag of the schools. There were twenty of these divisions. At the close of the procession was a body of thirty youths, each bearing a wand with a light pennon attached. These lads were to be employed as 'orderlies', marking the line of the procession along the roads and in the fields and aiding the main body to fall into order again when dispersed for recreation.

If any of the children were disposed, on their march around the districts of Stranmillis and Belvoir, to adopt too frivolous an approach to Easter Monday, they had the words of the morning service ringing in their ears, and even at the end of a long day were given little opportunity to stray from the true path when Dr Drew preached to them once more.

> He then called their attention to four subjects, Obedience, Correction, Penitence and Resignation and questioned the children on the history of Jonah as singularly illustrative of these points.

Despite these efforts the evangelical clergy did not sweep all before them. In 1845, 20,000 people still attended at the Cave Hill and as late as 1861 we find the *Northern Whig* describing Easter as 'a drunken festival'. If the direct appeal did not end the Cave Hill festivities there were more subtle ways of eroding them. As early as 1844 the writer of the Christ church annals noted with approval that:

> the proprietors of land in the neighbourhood, witnessing the great decrease of visitors, have refused admittance to those who may still present themselves, so that this noted place is likely to be no more defiled by such exhibitors as disgraced our community for many years.

This comment was premature in 1844 but by 1858 local landowners were ready to take advantage of the fair's decline. In that year a linen draper named Magill closed public access to the Cave Hill and the *Northern Whig* reported that, in response, 'a demonstration on the Cavehill is threatened'. Significantly, the demonstration did not take place and instead Magill was defeated in a celebrated court case, but Magill's ruin was a victory for middle class litigants and seekers after fresh air rather than the Easter Monday poteen drinkers who by then had moved elsewhere.

By the late 1840s attractive alternatives to the Cave Hill had developed. The Bangor steamers and the railways made it possible to leave the town, and within Belfast new venues such as the museum became available. However, the real successor to Cave Hill was Dargan's Island, later Queen's Island, an island of seventeen acres which had been created from the dredgings of the Victoria Channel and been laid out as a pleasure park. The facilities on the Island included a conservatory, a menagerie—Belfast's first zoo—

Queen's Island as shown in J. H. Connop's view of Belfast c. 1863 (Linenhall Library). Note the encroachment of Harland & Wolff's shipyard onto the pleasure ground.

with pheasants, parrots, a racoon, monkeys, and even a golden eagle. There was also an early amusement arcade, with penny-operated mechanical models including an executioner removing the head of Charles I, a master caning a pupil, a barrel organ and peep shows, featuring battles rather than bathing belles.

The Island was not purely an Easter venue, it was attractive throughout the summer, and indeed was immortalised in Belfast's most popular music hall song of the 1870s, 'The Solid Muldoon' by W. J. Ashcroft:

At Holywood and at Dargan's Island,
With merry friends I oft go there,
To enjoy the summer recreation,
And the refreshing Lagan air.

The popularity of the Island on Easter Monday encouraged special efforts from the lessee, who always endeavoured to earn more than the 1d ferry fare. So in 1852 we find 'daring feats performed by the corps physiques' and 'whole legions of minor amusements such as running in sacks and climbing greased poles.' Though the Island offered a more commercial and organised environment than the Cave Hill there was still room for spontaneity, in 1870 a correspondent noted: 'the amusements were of the usual kind, but the visitors enjoyed themselves more by running over the grounds forming "kissing rings" and other favourite amusements'. There too, as a reminder that links with the past had not been entirely broken, was McIlvenna the blind harper.

The demise of Queen's Island as a pleasure ground in the mid 1870s was rapid and the cause simple—the land was required for the rapidly expanding shipyard—a useful reminder of how industrial expansion removed recreational opportunities for the poor of the inner city. In the same period, that is between the 1840s and the 1870s, the two principal bathing places for the working classes, at Donegall Quay and the Long Strand, along the foreshore by the Newtownards Road, were also closed by the march of industrial progress.

The Botanic Gardens now became the principal venue for all classes on Easter Monday. In 1874 we find 'the gardens were crowded not only by the purely working classes who formerly frequented the Island, but by the higher classes of sight-seer.' Here the visitors were spectators rather than participants, the *Northern Whig* tells us that with 'a vast assemblage, embracing a great proportion of the lower orders it was occasionally difficult to preserve the most perfect decorum'. However with the assistance of police and pickets of soldiers social control was maintained. It was a far cry from the spontaneous assembly of the Cave Hill. In fifty years the tradition of the blind harper, the poteen booth, and the dancing

Interior of Batty's circus, Chichester Street, in use for an anti-O'Connell demonstration in January, 1841 (*The Repealer Repulsed*, Belfast, 1841).

to 'Hibernia's planxties' had been replaced by commercially organised spectacle.

Meanwhile the new urban and working class sub-culture of Belfast was producing more regular forms of entertainment. The earliest of these were the singing saloons. Typical was the New Harmonic Saloon, an annex of the Plough Hotel, first advertised in December 1832. Such early saloons were usually no more than extensions to existing inns, and the link with drink was a direct one. In his biography, S. M. Elliott, recalling the saloons of the 1850s noted that 'to hear banjo and bones you required to enter, sit down and call for a penny class of beer . . . you were required to lose no time in disseminating the contents of your glass'.

Inevitably many of these saloons were rough and bawdy. One correspondent describing the Oddfellows Hall in 1847 found: 'Disreputable female vocalists who dared show their brazen and drunken faces before the very lowest audience that could be collected in Belfast.' While most singing saloons catered only for the working classes, one or two provided facilities for more daring gentlemen. In 1848 we learn that the Robert Burns saloon in Long Lane provided 'a quiet snuggery which affords the greatest privacy' a measure necessary because if the well-to-do were noticed by the main audience they were likely to be made the object of ridicule.

Sam Cowell, who performed at Queen's Island, the Shakespeare Concert Hall and the Theatre Royal over the period 1849–1851 (Linenhall Library).

One singing saloon which aspired to greater things was the Shakespeare in Arthur Square, which flourished from 1841 until demolished to make way for the Theatre Royal in 1871. In 1850 the Shakespeare attracted Sam Cowell, a popular north of England entertainer, this was a great coup, and 'hundreds were turned away'. Cowell was also a summer attraction at Queen's Island, and sang at the theatre during intervals. But while entertainers might move freely between the theatre and the saloon, audiences did not. So in December 1841, when he wished to cater for 'the general desire amongst a number of respectable families to have an opportunity of hearing the performers whom he has engaged', the Shakespeare's proprietor hired the theatre.

The founding of the Alhambra, by Dan Lowrey in 1873, represented a departure. Lowrey was a concert hall entrepreneur who had achieved some success in Manchester and Liverpool, and clearly saw great opportunities in Belfast where the business had not yet escaped from the back rooms of taverns. Yet, in spite of his 'band of melodists—white men and niggers', he did not meet with the expected success, and in 1878 left for Dublin. He was still to make a significant impact on entertainment in Belfast, but for the moment he left the Alhambra in the hands of Willie John Ashcroft, a talented Irish-American comedian, who was to make the venue famous, indeed at times notorious, over the next twenty years.

Many rising stars of English music hall crossed the Alhambra stage, men like Charles Coburn, Dan Leno, and Harry Lauder. But there was also room for local songs, sometimes owing much to the native folk tradition, though more often the music hall featured adaptations of popular songs, such as Ashcroft's 'The Solid Muldoon', a rewritten version of a New York hit. Entertainment at the Alhambra did not lack variety, and on occasion included small boys dipping in barrels of tar for sixpences, or racing through hot apple dumplings with their hands tied behind their backs for similar prizes.

In spite of Ashcroft's very public private life—which included battles on stage with his wife, a scandalous court case, and periodic retreats to the lunatic asylum—or perhaps, in part, because of it, his enterprise flourished; evidence perhaps that working class audiences were much less interested in questions of morality than their clergy might have desired. Ashcroft's reign had an influence that went far beyond the Alhambra's doors. Dan Leno noted 'when we visited Mr Ashcroft at his saloon in Belfast, we spent all our time showing each other original steps and dancing against each other till people who see us must think us mad'. This enthusiasm for clog and step-dancing was a local peculiarity which lasted until the 1920s, and imitators of Ashcroft were also to far outlast their master as variety turns in the cinemas of the same period.

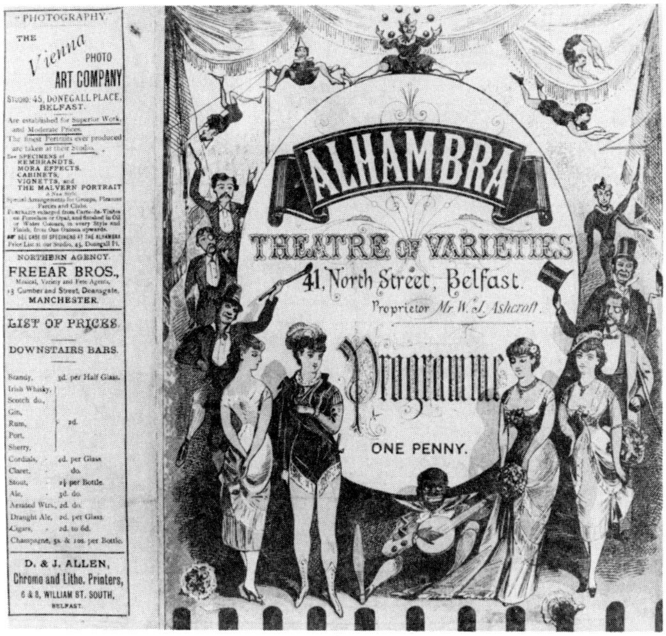

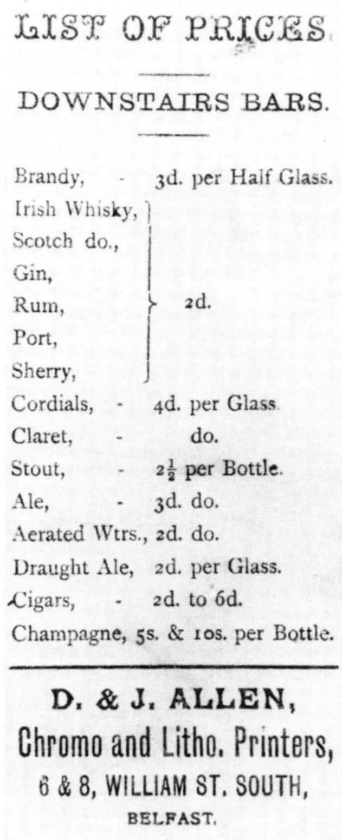

LIST OF PRICES.

DOWNSTAIRS BARS.

Brandy,	-	3d. per Half Glass.
Irish Whisky, Scotch do., Gin, Rum, Port, Sherry,		2d.
Cordials,	-	4d. per Glass.
Claret,	-	do.
Stout,	-	2½ per Bottle.
Ale,	-	3d. do.
Aerated Wtrs.,		2d. do.
Draught Ale,		2d. per Glass.
Cigars,	-	2d. to 6d.
Champagne,		5s. & 10s. per Bottle.

D. & J. ALLEN,
Chromo and Litho. Printers,
6 & 8, WILLIAM ST. SOUTH,
BELFAST.

Illustrated cover for an Alhambra programme of the 1880s; bar prices at the Alhambra (Central Library).

The first real threat to the Alhambra came with the opening of the Olympia Palace in 1891, on the site of the present Grand Opera House. Mr. Barnard, the proprietor, determined to set a new tone: he announced 'everything associated with the old fashioned vulgarity of the music halls is rigidly excluded' and spoke instead of 'variety'. Though Barnard did not survive for long, 'variety', or bowdlerised

Poster dated 1869 for Dr Corry's diorama, one of the most successful of the predecessors of modern cinema (Central Library).

music hall, with its broadly-based appeal, and power to draw large, all-class audiences was an ideal vehicle for the entrepreneurs of the entertainment world. And it was Dan Lowrey, who had failed at the Alhambra, then made a fortune with the Star Music Hall in Dublin, who now, at the head of a syndicate, returned to Belfast offering variety.

The site for their new venture, in Victoria Square, had a long singing saloon tradition. Here had stood the Buffalo with its annex 'where the well-to-do could avoid the abuse of the gallery'; and later the New Colosseum. Now an extravagant Moorish palace, the Empire Theatre of Varieties, arose on the site and opened in 1894.

The Empire attracted an entirely new audience. For the first time women could attend without fear of reproach, and the lavish interior overcame the qualms of the business classes. At the same time the Empire directly threatened the working class audience of the Alhambra, which now found it difficult to attract the best artistes because the variety chains, including the Empire, were signing them up on exclusive contracts. Symptomatic of the rapid changes in the organisation and technology of entertainment towards the end of the century was the showing of the first films in Belfast at the Alhambra and the Empire in 1896. There were significant predecessors to the cinematograph, notably diorama; indeed Belfast was the birthplace of one of the most successful of these entertainments, Dr. Corry's National Diorama of Ireland, which was first displayed at the Victoria Hall in 1864, and subsequently toured England, America and Australia. This consisted of fifty views of Ireland painted on 20' x 12' canvases, and illuminated to the accompaniment of romantic Irish melodies sung by Nellie Hayes 'the Irish nightingale', who performed dressed as a colleen. Local versifier Barney Maglone paid tribute to the popularity of Dr Corry's diorama:

We have in Belfast now that sprig of the dhrama,
That high flying people must call 'diorama',
The manin' of that is a great congregation,
Of pitchers that show the old spots of the nation,
The ould spots—the sweet spots, the spots that can still,
To the eyes give delight, to the heart give a thrill,
An along with the pitchers there's courtin galore,
An sich singing—I'm bate—I can tell you no more.

Another form of live entertainment which achieved lasting popularity in the city was the circus. Circuses were primarily travelling entertainments, but proved so successful in Belfast that occasionally permanent premises were taken. In the late 1830s Batty's circus had premises in Chichester Street capable of seating over 1,000 spectators. Iater in the century the site of the Grand Opera House played host to a succession of travelling circuses such as Cooke's Ginnet's and Hengler's, and even with the construction of the Opera

House this tradition was not wholly abandoned, with the words 'and cirque' being added to the name of the new theatre.

The popularity of the circus did not pass unnoticed. The *Northern Whig* in 1855 commented 'it is a curious feature in connection with the taste of the Belfast public that few entertainments "take" better than equestrianism'. A clue to the popularity of circus lies in an advertisement for Pablo Fanque's Circus Royal of 1851, which began by noting 'Public amusements are but too often conducted in a manner regardless of the morals of the visitors', and went on to assure all that, at Pablo Fanque's, 'so cautious will be the selection, that the tender father, the affectionate husband, or admiring lover need not fear the blush of modesty.' Circus offered simple and moral entertainment in a period in which the traditional stage was almost emptied by clerical assault.

Of all entertainments it was the theatre which suffered the most chequered career in the nineteenth century, and this despite a distinguished past. Travelling companies from Dublin and further afield had found Belfast a fruitful venue in the early eighteenth century. By 1784 the growing town had a permanent theatre, and visiting stars such as Sarah Siddons roused the northern elite to almost hysterical enthusiasm. In 1793, a new theatre was constructed in Arthur Square, and during the first decade of the new century this had the support of Belfast's business and leisured classes.

The period after the Napoleonic Wars was marked by considerable social tension and the theatre did not prove immune. In 1819 an actress was severely injured by a stone thrown from the gallery. It is clear that this incident was not an isolated one, for in the following year, the theatre manager had to call on the sovereign of the town to provide officers to patrol the theatre. Clearly violence discouraged the clientele who had been the mainstay of the theatre—the gentry, but there were more subtle reasons for their disengagement. The *Northern Whig* in 1827 noted that whereas in the past the elite had applauded with enthusiasm, now people of rank sat 'with the icy coldness and frigid precision of statues' fearing identification with 'the coarse approbation of the gods, or the unpolished demonstrations of approval resorted to by shopkeepers and tradesmen'. Thackeray provided a useful description of the mid-Victorian audience when he visited Belfast in 1842. It was typical of the times that his gentleman host 'had never been in the playhouse (and) he had never heard of anyone going thither'. He found 'a party of six in the boxes, the benches of the pit being dotted over with about a score or more'. By contrast 'the gallery was quite full, and exceedingly happy and noisy.'

However, more significant than the withdrawal of the well-to-do was the way in which the theatre was fixed on by the clergy in their campaign to cleanse Belfast society. Perhaps the most notorious incident in this campaign occurred in 1844, when a member of the

Illustrated poster for an evening of melodrama at the Theatre Royal in 1868 (Central Library). David Allen, the printer, commenced business in 1857 and by 1900 had the largest theatrical printing business in the world.

military garrison at Carrickfergus, John Cordery, attended the theatre, got drunk, and on returning to barracks murdered his sergeant. Cordery was the last man to be publicly executed in Carrickfergus and at the scaffold he repented that he had ever darkened the door of the theatre.

The clergy, led by a prominent Church of Ireland minister, Dr Drew, were not slow to make capital out of the event. They even petitioned the commander in chief of the Irish garrison to prevent amateurs from the garrison undertaking a charitable performance in aid of the Frederick Street hospital. This effort failed but the impact of their opposition to the theatre was lasting and acutely damaging.

With the Belfast theatre, or Theatre Royal (as it was known from the 1840s) under seige, it is perhaps surprising that a number of competitors emerged. One of the most interesting of these was Mr Heffernan's National Theatre which opened in 1848, with the worthy object of 'giving the poorer classes the same opportunity as their more wealthy neighbours of seeing the drama'. With rock bottom prices and twice nightly performances Heffernan temporarily prospered, his clientele extending beyond the working classes to 'the better class of tradesmen and their families', but his business was destroyed by the cholera epidemic of 1849. The only thing that saved the Theatre Royal in the same period was that it was leased by successive managers, so their various bankruptcies did not lead to the demise of the premises.

When in 1864 Mr J. F. Warden became manager of the Theatre Royal he faced rather better prospects. After the slowed growth of the 1840s and early 1850s, Belfast's economy was recovering and the population was growing rapidly. With rising incomes, and the emergence of a skilled working class, theatre-going was now within the means of a larger proportion of an increased population. In addition, the development of the railways, with efficient late night services that would be of credit to railways today made it possible for people from up to fifty miles away to come to Belfast for the evening.

Like managers before him Warden was an actor, and his wife, Jenny Bellairs, was an actress. He was also an astute businessman, as can be seen from the delicate adjustments he made to his seating arrangements in 1865, scrapping his dress boxes to create a more democratic dress circle, and later renaming the area the lower circle, in an effort to maximize the appeal of his higher-priced seats.

The proceedings, however, were as rough and uproarious as previously. There was no system of queuing so when the doors opened it was a free-for-all and often a battle. At intervals amateurs in the audience sang and on occasion they were so reluctant to leave the stage that it was a time before the performance could be resumed. This audience was noted for fierce loyalties rather than any particular taste, thus the celebrated mid-Victorian actor G. V. Brooke remained a Belfast favourite in his later years although a chronic alcoholic and debarred from other provincial theatres. On one famous occasion Brooke fell asleep while playing the lead role in *Richelieu*, and a near riot ensued as part of the audience demanded that the performance stop, and the gods, with equal vigour, insisted that all should wait until Brooke awoke.

As a result of improved economic circumstances, good financial management and a caution in repertoire, the theatre's prosperity increased. So much so that in 1869 Warden faced exorbitant demands for the renewal of his lease. Fortunately other businessmen in the city saw the potential of his enterprise and backed the

The second Theatre Royal, after the disastrous fire of 1881 (Welch Collection, Ulster Museum).

construction of a New Theatre Royal. This opened in 1871, and its facade spoke much of its pretensions. Here were arches of polished Aberdeen granite, Cookstown, Whitehaven and Portland stone, all ornamented with Shakespearian sculptures. And when this theatre was destroyed by fire in 1881 it was replaced by an even grander edifice.

The sophistication of the audience did not advance correspondingly; indeed the opening night at the second Theatre Royal was almost destroyed by uproar from the gods. Rowdyism as a response to a dull play was one thing, but potential theatre-goers absented themselves or demonstrated for more considered reasons. In 1881 Sarah Bernhardt played to half empty houses because her French play was considered 'immoral' and, as if this was not enough, was in 'a foreign language'. In the early 1890s, when Sir Frank

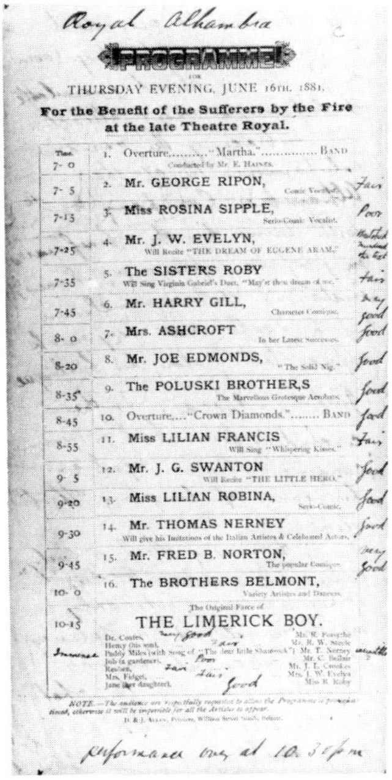
PROGRAMME
FOR
THURSDAY EVENING, JUNE 16TH, 1881.
For the Benefit of the Sufferers by the Fire at the late Theatre Royal.

Time.		
7- 0	1.	Overture........"Martha."............ BAND Conducted by Mr. E. Haines.
7- 5	2.	Mr. GEORGE RIPON, Comic Vocalist.
7-15	3.	Miss ROSINA SIPPLE, Serio-Comic Vocalist.
7-25	4.	Mr. J. W. EVELYN, Will Recite "THE DREAM OF EUGENE ARAM."
7-35	5.	The SISTERS ROBY Will Sing Virginia Gabriel's Duet, "May'st thou dream of me."
7-45	6.	Mr. HARRY GILL, Character Comique.
8- 0	7.	Mrs. ASHCROFT In her Latest Successes.
8-20	8.	Mr. JOE EDMONDS, "The Solid Nig."
8-35	9.	The POLUSKI BROTHER,S The Marvellous Grotesque Acrobats.
8-45	10.	Overture,..."Crown Diamonds."........ BAND
8-55	11.	Miss LILIAN FRANCIS Will Sing "Whispering Kisses."
9- 5	12.	Mr. J. G. SWANTON Will Recite "THE LITTLE HERO."
9-20	13.	Miss LILIAN ROBINA, Serio-Comic.
9-30	14.	Mr. THOMAS NERNEY Will give his Imitations of the Italian Artistes & Celebrated Actors.
9-45	15.	Mr. FRED B. NORTON, The popular Comique.
10- 0	16.	The BROTHERS BELMONT, Variety Artistes and Dancers.
10-15		The Original Farce of THE LIMERICK BOY.

Programme for a benefit held at the Alhambra for the actors of the Theatre Royal, after the 1881 fire (Central Library). The performance was successful, W. J. Lawrence records that 'the hall was crowded in every part, standing room itself being almost unavailable.

Benson first performed his uncensored version of *Richard III*, the audience revealed their resistance to change by stopping the performance with cries of 'bring back Barry Sullivan', a reference to a favourite performer of the familiar Colley Cibber version.

The theatre was changing in other respects too. From the 1870s, when the great travelling companies came into their own, provincial theatre managers became in effect, mere lessees of their premises to these companies. The arrangement certainly left little room for in-house originality, and Belfast's local stock company was disbanded. One useful consequence, however, was that objections on moral grounds eased, for whatever the play, local doubters could be assured that the English bourgeoisie had seen and approved of it first.

The return of Belfast high society to the theatre was particularly noticeable in the field of opera. This was not surprising because even in the period when theatre was viewed as anathema, Belfast's leading families had never lost their enthusiasm for music. Now at the Theatre Royal they flocked to see the Carl Rosa, Moody Manners, and D'Oyly Carte companies. The theatre historian W. J. Lawrence, describing a visit of the Carl Rosa company in May 1881 noted 'the house was crowded in every part, the dress circle including most of the elite of Northern society'.

The theatre was also quite successful in winning a new working class audience. Writing in 1891 the actor Whitford Kane recorded that the Royal's gallery included 'shipyard workers in their dungarees, men from the linen and rope factories, shawled mill girls, clerks old and young, and stage-struck apothecary apprentices like myself.' Particularly important here was the pantomime, the one area in which Warden continued to act as manager and impresario,

Sarah Bernhardt, from a collection of postcards recording the stars who visited Belfast, assembled by W. Barrington-Baker (Central Library).

taking his pantomimes to Dublin, Cork and Liverpool; leading Lawrence to disdainfully note in 1891 that his entertainments were 'quite as appropriate to the music hall as the theatre'. This success was, however, far from comprehensive. Harry Furniss, writing in *Black and White* in 1891, and noting the city had 'only one theatre where there might be two,' observed 'It is true that people do not go to the theatre in Belfast. There are those who would as soon visit the infernal regions.'

The arrival of the Grand Opera House, in 1895, which presented the best of English artistes and productions, confirmed the theatre's return to respectability, after a century of chequered fortune. The reasons for its eclipse have already been gone into but it is difficult, before concluding, to resist the speculation that its decline may have had much to do with the nature of its audience. It may have been that those bulwarks of the theatre, the fashionable and well-to-do, were more affected by the moral conservatism of mid-Victorian Belfast than the classes who took their pleasures at the music halls.

Since the beginning of the century the nature of these pleasures had undergone significant changes. The traditional and participatory entertainments of the countryside were lost in the process of urbanisation, which in turn eliminated the natural recreation and pleasure grounds convenient to working class areas. Rising incomes and particularly the emergence of a skilled working class, a very marked feature of Belfast society, created new possibilities and entertainment became an industry. Until the 1870s the local market was catered for by local entrepreneurs, with minimal capital. But when improvements in transport—first the introduction of the steamship, and then the rapid growth of the railways—made possible the regular and easy movement of artistes from England to Ireland, and later the transit of gigantic companies on complicated schedules throughout the United Kingdom, this era came to an end.

The full flowering of this uni-cultural merry-go-round could not occur until local entrepreneurs had developed their market to a point which enabled them to provide the touring companies with the appropriate facilities. In Belfast this progression occurred well within the working lives of the first generation of substantial entrepreneurs. Its main requirement was a large audience, and both in the theatre and elsewhere this helped to dictate the nature of the entertainment, with an emphasis on blandness rather than bawdiness, and the use of entertainments which had proved successful elsewhere rather than local experiment. As the new century dawned the ascendancy of variety and the revived theatre seemed complete. But the next revolution had already begun, and with the showing of films as variety turns from 1896 on, the variety colossus unwittingly encouraged the next major change in popular entertainment, the coming of the cinema, and this was to be a revolution which would sweep all before it.

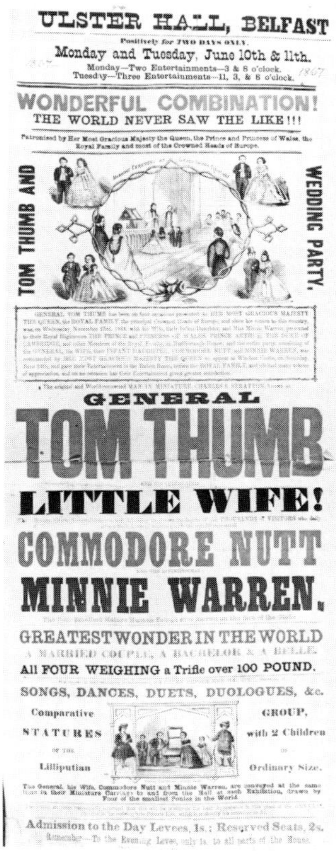

'General Tom Thumb' and Family visited the Ulster Hall at the height of their fame in 1867 (Central Library) They had previously appeared as relative unknowns at the Theatre Royal; a reminder that freak shows were a popular Victorian entertainment.

8. Religion and secular thought 1800–75

Peter Brooke

In 1874, the British Association for the Advancement of Science met in Belfast. The British Association met each year in a different town with a different president, to hear a wide range of papers summing up the year's advances in scientific thought. The president in 1874 was John Tyndall, an engineer and geologist, who already had a reputation as an opponent of religious interference in scientific matters.

In his presidential address, Tyndall gave an excited and wide ranging account of the materialist world view (though he rejected the term 'materialism'). He traced the theory that the world had developed through the interplay of atoms back to Democritus; argued that consciousness was not known to exist except as an attribute of matter, that religious preconceptions could only be an obstacle to scientific thought, and that it was possible to discern in matter 'the promise and potency of every form and quality of life'.

The address soon became famous throughout Europe and provoked a wide variety of replies. Among them were two by ministers in Belfast, the Rev. Dr Watts, professor of systematic theology in Assembly's College; and the Rev. Dr John Scott Porter, minister of the second presbyterian congregation, Rosemary Street. The arguments in both pamphlets were similar and not especially remarkable. Each contended, in effect, that natural phenomena were so well designed that there must have been a designer. Both writers emphasised that they were very well disposed towards science, indeed, Watts had prepared *An Irenicum, or A Plea for Peace and Co-operation between Science and Theology* and was clearly resentful that it had been rejected by the Association which had given Tyndall a platform from which to launch, in the name of science, an attack on religion.

Watts and Porter represented opposite extremes of religious thought in Belfast. Watts was a rigorously orthodox adherent of the Westminster Confession of Faith, and a man respected throughout the presbyterian world as an unbending opponent of fashionable, secularising ideas. Porter was a unitarian and a member of the Northern Presbytery of Antrim, which refused to subscribe to any creed or confession of faith. At the time of Tyndall's address, the school of thought represented by Watts was in the ascendant among

John Tyndall in 1873. (*The life and work of John Tyndall*, Eve and Creasey, London, 1945).

the presbyterians of Belfast. Yet, in the small town of the eighteenth century, two of the three presbyterian churches (all of them in Rosemary Street) were non-subscribing, and the initiative for the town's first major centre of learning—the Belfast Academical Institution—had come largely from non-subscribers.

The Academical Institution was both a school and a college of higher education, and was based on the principle that education should take place in the context of a generalised Christianity that was common to all the major denominations. As far as school level education was concerned there was at the beginning of the century little disagreement over this principle. Henry Cooke and James Morgan, leaders of orthodox presbyterian opinion in Belfast, were both taught by Roman Catholic schoolmasters, while Gavan Duffy, who pioneered the development of catholic politics in Belfast, was taught by presbyterians. The contemporary 'Kildare Place Society' was supporting a large number of non-sectarian primary schools throughout the country, though a quarrel was soon to blow up as to whether or not the Bible, as a freely available text book, could be regarded as a part of this common Christianity.

In the 1820s, however, orthodox opinion in the presbyterian Synod of Ulster increasingly felt that the non-sectarianism of the collegiate department was favourable to unitarianism, which was increasingly being avowed by the leading non-subscribers. From the 1820s until it closed in 1849, the department was plagued by problems of the interaction between religious and secular education.

By the time of the British Association meeting these had been separated out into two major centres of learning in Belfast—Queen's College (later Queen's University) and the presbyterian Assembly's

THE SCIENTIFIC VOLUNTEER.

"If ever I have to choose .... I shall, without hesitation, shoulder my rifle with the Orangeman."—*See Professor Tyndall's Reply to Sir W. V. Harcourt.* "*Times*," Feb. 13, 1890.

A cartoon from *Punch*. Tyndall, a native of Co. Carlow, was to become an enthusiastic unionist.

College. Methodist College had opened in 1868, and had a collegiate department for trainee ministers, but this was on a very small scale. Belfast was recognised as first and foremost a presbyterian town, and, until the disestablishment of the Church of Ireland in 1870, Assembly's College received a government grant. Religion was excluded from the curriculum of Queen's College, but its first two presidents, Pooley Shuldam Henry and Josias Leslie Porter, were presbyterian ministers. It was the (non-denominational) college for presbyterians as Cork and Galway were supposed to be the (non-denominational) colleges for Roman Catholics. Did this presbyterianism obstruct the development of an intellectual life that was not based on religion? What influence did it have on the development of institutions of higher education and on political, philosophical and scientific thinking in the nineteenth century?

The disputes over the collegiate department of the Academical Institution could be said to have centred round the distinction between religious and secular knowledge. Were Greek and Hebrew secular subjects, given that they were the languages of the Bible? What about moral philosophy? If these were branches of divinity, should the Synod not exercise some control over the way they were taught? It must be borne in mind when looking at these disputes that

The Rev. John Scott Porter, oil painting by Richard Rothwell (Ulster Museum).

the great majority of the students in the Institution's collegiate department were candidates for the presbyterian ministry. It was primarily a theological seminary, though it aspired to be a centre for secular studies. The surprising thing was the extent to which the Synod at first accepted that its authority would be limited to one specialist subject—divinity—and that all other knowledge should be regarded as secular and outside its control.

Throughout the twenties, Henry Cooke tried to persuade the Synod that Greek and Hebrew were not religiously neutral subjects and that there were dangers in allowing ministers to be taught by professors with heterodox views on the Doctrine of the Trinity. But even after the unitarians had left the Synod in 1829 Cooke's campaign against the Institution had still produced little more than expressions of concern (and this relative indifference was shared, even more surprisingly, by the more orthodox Secession Synod). The Synod did not insist on carrying its authority beyond the Divinity Faculty until the 1830s, when the issue was not Greek or Hebrew, but moral philosophy.

Professor John Ferrie, appointed professor of moral philosophy in 1829, was not a unitarian or a philosophical radical. He belonged to a long tradition of Scottish philosophical thinking which had flowered into the utilitarianism of James Mill and Jeremy Bentham and which tended to explain moral behaviour and social interaction without recourse to the teaching of the Bible (this tradition, incidentally, owed much to an Ulsterman, the great eighteenth-century philosopher, Francis Hutcheson). The Synod complained that Ferrie was ignoring the doctrines of sin and the need for salvation, and withdrew its students from his classes, establishing its own moral philosophy classes, at first under Henry Cooke and William Molyneaux. In this way, they were expanding their authority outside the Divinity Faculty. (But at the same time, they were also expanding the Divinity Faculty itself through the addition of chairs in Biblical criticism and ecclesiastical history.)

The original thinking behind the Faculty had been that it would comprise professors from all the major denominations. In fact it had merely consisted of professors from the two orthodox presbyterian bodies—the Synod of Ulster and the Secession Synod. In 1840, however, the two unitarian bodies—the Remonstrant Synod (formed in 1830 by the non-subscribing ministers who had left the Synod of Ulster) and the long established Presbytery of Antrim successfully applied to the college to accept their respective nominees, Henry Montgomery and John Scott Porter. Rather than co-operate with unitarians, the orthodox professors withdrew and became a peripatetic faculty divorced from the Institution. The demand for a separate college fully under the control of the General Assembly (formed from the union of the Synod of Ulster and the Seceders in 1840) became a central feature of presbyterian politics, and finally issued in the establishment of Assembly's College in Belfast (1853), and Magee College in Londonderry (1865).

Assembly's College, Belfast (*The Presbyterian College, Belfast 1853–1953*, Robert Allen, Belfast, 1954).

It should be said that this refusal to co-operate with unitarians was by no means peculiar to Belfast. The great Arian controversy in Belfast in the 1820s had been preceded by the controversy between Wardlaw and Yates in Glasgow. The 'Manchester Socinian Controversy' took place at the same time as the Belfast controversy. The typical English form of the controversy was a demand from the orthodox that unitarians were not entitled to property originally endowed for orthodox purposes. In the 1830s, unitarians were expelled from the 'Protestant Dissenting Deputies' which had been formed in London to represent the purely secular political interests of dissenters, but which was now turning to the attack on unitarian property. The quarrel over property was a dominant feature in Ulster too in the 1830s, and the whole issue was only resolved in 1844 with Peel's Dissenters Chapels Act, which came down on the side of the unitarians. The most peculiar feature of the Ulster situation was that although all the major Christian churches (including, of course, the established churches of England and Ireland) anathematised unitarianism as anti-Christian, the Remonstrant Synod and the Presbytery of Antrim continued to receive government support (in the form of 'regium donum') even after their unitarianism had become explicit.

The Institution had started life under the suspicion of being a potential centre for radical politics owing to the participation, in the early years, of several people associated with the United Irish movement of the 1790s—most notably Dr William Drennan, Dr Robert Tennent, and W. B. Neilson. Neilson, who died young, was a son of Samuel Neilson, editor of the United Irish paper, the *Northern Star*. At the time of the Institution's establishment Drennan was editor of the *Belfast Monthly Magazine*, a paper which, while condemning Napoleon as a tyrant, nonetheless opposed the government for its alliance with reactionary forces ranged against him. Tennent was the brother of William Tennent, who had been imprisoned for complicity in the rising.

Tennent's son, Robert James Tennent, who was a pupil of the Institution, was a member in the 1820s of John Stuart Mill's London Debating Society, and his papers from this period reflect a wide ranging interest in the major ideas of the time, from 'political economy' to the socialism of Robert Owen. Together with his friend James Emerson, he went on a romantic expedition, following Byron, to help liberate Greece from the Turks. The two stood against each other in the 1832 election in Belfast and Emerson won, subsequently to become a Peelite Tory and governor of Ceylon.

The Institution also had as students three of the most remarkable radical newspaper editors of their time: James Simms, editor of the *Northern Whig*; James MacNeight, editor of the *Londonderry Standard* and of the Belfast-based *Banner of Ulster*; and Gavan Duffy, editor of the Young Ireland paper, *The Nation*, who enrolled in the school of logic, rhetoric and belles-lettres for a short period in the early 1840s.

Duffy was a Roman Catholic from County Monaghan who had contributed to the Belfast-based *Northern Herald*, which was edited between 1834 and 1835 by Thomas O'Hagan (another of the Institution's students) who was later to become the first Roman Catholic lord chancellor of Ireland. The *Northern Herald* supported the repeal of the union, in opposition to the *Northern Whig*, which was enthusiastic about the political possibilities opened up by the 1832 Reform Bill. Duffy went on to edit *The Vindicator,* started in

James Emerson Tennent, elected MP for Belfast with Lord Arthur Chichester after the 1832 Reform Act (Ulster Museum).

1839 to continue the *Herald's* work of developing a distinct Roman Catholic political voice in Belfast. He moved to Dublin in 1842. The 'League of North and South', as Duffy christened the tenant right movement of the late '40s/early '50s, was largely a league between Duffy and James MacNeight.

MacNeight had played a leading part in opposing the old radical Reform Association and in the forming of the Belfast Society, to support James Emerson in the 1832 election. He left it, however, as it developed into the Belfast Conservative Society, largely under the influence of Henry Cooke, who had moved to Belfast in 1829. The *Banner of Ulster*, which MacNeight edited between 1848 and 1853, had been founded by William Gibson, the Synod of Ulster's professor of moral philosophy, and later the historian of the 1859 Revival, to articulate a distinctly orthodox presbyterian political interest—against the unitarians and the Dissenters Chapels Bill; against the claims of the Church of Ireland; and in favour of a college for the education of presbyterian ministers that would be completely in the hands of the Presbyterian Church.

By the 1850s, however, when MacNeight returned to the *Londonderry Standard*, the centre of presbyterian radicalism had moved west of the Bann. Both the orthodox Henry Cooke and the unitarian Henry Montgomery had, while acknowledging the grievances on which the tenant right movement was based, opposed the activities of the movement led by Duffy and MacNeight. Belfast, largely under Cooke's influence, had also accepted an arrangement by which the education of its ministers was separated into an arts

Henry Cooke in later life (*The Presbyterian College, Belfast 1853–1953*, Robert Allen, Belfast, 1954).

course in the Queen's College, under government control, and a theology course in Assembly's College under the control of the General Assembly. This division was rejected by Londonderry, which finally achieved the establishment of a college wholly in presbyterian hands when Magee College was opened in 1865.

Duffy's politics in *The Vindicator* were distinctly catholic even if his support for the non-sectarian Queen's Colleges, proposed by Peel in 1845, was to lead him, together with the rest of the Young Ireland movement, into conflict with O'Connell and most of the catholic hierarchy. (The exceptions included the primate, William Crolly, formerly parish priest of Belfast, who, by 1845 was completely out of sympathy with the militant sectarianism of his church.) MacNeight's politics, of course, were distinctly presbyterian. But despite the attack on unitarianism, there were significant differences between the presbyterian politics of Belfast and nonconformist politics in England or Scotland. Although they were engaged in controversy on several fronts with the Church of Ireland, the Belfast presbyterians were not prepared to go the lengths of opposing church establishments in principle, the position that was increasingly becoming general both among the presbyterian dissenters in Scotland and congregationalist dissenters in England. There was an attempt to establish a Belfast Voluntary Church Association in the 1830s, but this was based for the most part on members of small sects which received no government aid. The ministers of the main presbyterian denominations stood to lose half their salary if the voluntary principle (by which churches were to be supported solely by voluntary contributions from their members) was adopted. Thus, although Henry Cooke's idea of a 'protestant

Union' between the Presbyterian Church and the Church of Ireland was rejected—to the extent that Cooke refused to attend the General Assembly from 1843 to 1847—the attack on the Church of Ireland fell short of an alliance with the formidable anti-establishment movement that had gathered in Great Britain.

We have some idea, then, of how religious attitudes affected the development of the institutions of higher education, the teaching of moral philosophy, and the development of political ideas. But what of the development of a scientific view of the world, the subject of Tyndall's lecture?

By 1874, science had brushed with religion on several fronts. Most directly, the development of historiography had raised questions both as to the authenticity of the Bible text, and the accuracy of its account of Jewish history. The critical study of the Bible as a historical and literary text had received a new impetus in Germany in the first half of the nineteenth century and contributed, together with Hegel's ambitious attempt at an all-embracing philosophy, to the ferment of ideas out of which Marxism was to develop. Belfast, like the rest of the British Isles, despite the best efforts of Coleridge and Carlyle, was fairly well insulated from German thinking at least until the 1850s, by which time, partly in reaction to the failure of the 1848 revolutions, religious belief was re-establishing its intellectual ascendancy in the German universities.

Assembly's College, while Dr Watts was professor of theology, was well known for its resistance to any Biblical criticism which did not reach traditionally orthodox conclusions. After the 'disruption' of 1843, when the Church of Scotland was divided into the Established Church and the Free Church, the Irish General Assembly gave its support to the more traditionalist Free Church. In 1880, William

Dr Robert Watts, professor of systematic theology, Assembly's College (from *The Presbyterian College, Belfast 1853–1953*, by Robert Allen, Belfast, 1954).

Robertson Smith, professor of Old Testament Hebrew and exegesis in Free Church College, Aberdeen, was tried for heresy because he endorsed some of the doubts cast by Biblical criticism in an article on 'the Bible' in the 1875 edition of the *Encyclopaedia Britannica.* He was acquitted, though deprived of his professorship in 1881 for an article on Hebrew language and literature. Watts joined in the attack on him. The conservative Free Presbyterians, who broke from the Free Church in 1892, because of what they saw as the slackening of confessional standards, continued to send their students to Assembly's College until Watts died in 1895.

Nonetheless Belfast—and orthodox Belfast at that—did produce one of the most notable Bible critics of the time, Samuel Davidson. Davidson—a native of Kellswater, near Ballymena—was appointed professor of Biblical criticism for the Synod in 1835 and was also editor of the *Orthodox Presbyterian,* published by the Synod as a weapon in the battle against unitarianism. In 1839 he published his *Lectures on Biblical Criticism,* and in 1842, thoroughly out of sympathy with the Synod and inclining to congregationalist views, he moved to England where he was to become well known as a translator and interpreter of German theology. In 1857 his views on the inspiration of the Bible and on the Mosaic composition of the Pentateuch produced a widespread controversy, and led to his being

Samuel Davidson, historian of the Bible, in later life (*The Presbyterian College, Belfast 1853–1953,* Robert Allen, Belfast, 1954).

forced to resign from his position as professor of Biblical literature and ecclesiastical history at Lancashire Independent College, Manchester. He was later to sit on the committee which, in 1884, published the revised version of the Old Testament.

The other major area in which there was a conflict between scientific and theological thought was the study of the origins both of geological formations and of life forms. Geology argued that the world was much older than the Biblical account seemed to suggest; while the study of natural history led to the development of a theory for the evolution of life forms which dispensed with the need for special acts of creation.

Until the middle of the nineteenth century it had been easy to assume that natural history was virtually a branch of theology. Nearly all protestant clergymen, including presbyterians, had been raised on William Paley's *Natural Theology or Evidences of the Existence and Attributes of the Deity* (1802), and bishop Butler's *Analogy of Religion Natural and Revealed* (1736), which argued that the ingenuity of the natural order was proof that it had been planned by a supernatural intelligence. Thus, to study the natural order was in a sense to study the mind of God. In his *Plea for Peace and Co-operation between Science and Theology,* before he was so rudely awakened by Tyndall's presidential address, Watts had described Kepler, Newton, Dalton, Faraday, Tyndall and Andrews (Thomas Andrews, vice-president of Queen's College, Belfast) as 'theological pioneers'.

The theory of evolution upset the world of Paley and Butler because it suggested a mechanism whereby a large part of the material world could be explained without the intervention of a creator. It also argued that there must have been continuous life on earth for much longer than the 6000 or so years suggested by a literal interpretation of the Bible. The theory, sketched out by Erasmus Darwin and Lamarck, was given a popular expression in the *Vestiges of Creation* published anonymously in 1844 by Robert Chambers (which, incidentally, contains the observation that the poorest inhabitants of Down and Antrim 'exhibit peculiar features of the most repulsive kind, projecting jaws with large open mouths, depressed noses, high cheek bones, and bowed legs, together with extremely diminutive stature.' It contrasts them in this respect with the beauty of the English upper classes.)

Chambers was answered by a Scottish writer, Hugh Miller, in 1849, in his *Footprints of the Creator,* which tried to reconcile a literal acceptance of the Bible with the uncomfortable new arguments being advanced by the scientists. In particular, it suggested that the six days of creation in Genesis represented ages of unknown and indefinite length, and argued that the evolution of one species into another was impossible, but that each species was itself the result of a separate act of creation. In 1859, in his *Thoughts on the Revival of 1859,* the minister of Fisherwick presbyterian church, James Morgan, wrote of the problems posed by science (especially geology) as having been solved by Miller's triumphant refutation of the *Vestiges.* 1859, year of the Ulster Revival, was also the year when Charles Darwin's *Origin of the Species* was published.

Belfast shared in the great interest in geology and natural history

Belfast Naturalists Field Club at the Giant's Causeway (Welch Collection, Ulster Museum).

that was typical of the period, and, even independently of the Institution and of the Queen's College it had its own library, which included a collection of scientific books; a Natural History and Philosophical Society, whose members opened the Botanic Gardens in 1827 and the College Square museum in 1831; and later, in 1863, the Belfast Naturalists Field Club, which arranged local geological and botanical excursions. There were a number of remarkable individuals active in the town over these years including, at the beginning of the century, John Templeton, who collected a little botanical garden at his house in Cranmore, and later, Robert Patterson, author of a number of standard school text books on zoology, and Thomas Workman, who became an expert on Malaysian spiders, some varieties of which were named after him.

The outstanding scientist produced by Belfast during the century was, of course, Sir William Thomson, Lord Kelvin, who was chief consultant on the laying of the transatlantic cable, successfully completed in 1866, and who also did valuable work on heat and electricity. Thomson, however, had left Belfast at the age of eleven to study in Glasgow, where his father, who had been professor of mathematics in the Institution, had taken a chair in 1832. William's brother, also called James, was professor of engineering in Queen's College from 1854–73, when he took the chair of civil engineering in Glasgow. Like his brother, James Thomson made important contributions to the understanding of thermodynamics, some of which were first communicated in papers read before the Belfast Natural History and Philosophical Society.

Perhaps the most impressive of the Queen's College professors, however, was Thomas Andrews, who spent his whole career in Belfast, as professor of chemistry at the Institution, then as vice-

Lord Kelvin, James Thomson, and their sister, Mrs Elizabeth King (grandmother of Ramsay MacDonald), from a chalk drawing by Agnes Gardiner King (National Portrait Gallery, London).

president and professor of chemistry at Queen's. He was impressive both as a college administrator and for his work on thermodynamics and the nature of the atmosphere. He belonged to a tradition of medical doctors who made important contributions to the intellectual life of the town. In the political sphere these included Drennan and Tennent, and James McDonnell, who had been associated in the 1790s with the United Irish movement. McDonnell pioneered the provision of medical facilities for the poor, as did James Lawson Drummond, who was the driving force behind the formation of the Belfast Natural History and Philosophical Society. Another key figure was Henry McCormac, who came to prominence as a young man through his observations on cholera, gathered in the great epidemic of 1832. He was largely responsible with Drummond, for the establishment of a medical school in the Institution in 1835. The cholera epidemics of 1816, 1832, and 1847 gave great impetus to the improvement of Belfast's medical facilities, and to research into the nature of the disease, as well as to the pressure for improved sanitation which was to be associated with A. G. Malcolm and Samuel Browne.

For the most part this scientific research and interest, both at amateur and professional level, proceeded within the Paley-ite assumption that the study of nature was the study of the works of God. The Vestiges controversy, however, which occurred at the time Queen's College was being established, had produced an awareness of the possibility of contention. James Thomson Jr, for example, complained that if the author of the Vestiges:

> gives his assent to the existence of God as a First Cause, he at least

Dr Henry McCormac (Ulster Museum).

> supposes him to be now infinitely removed from all the works of nature, and that everything goes on now of itself just as a clock goes after its weights have been wound up.

In 1855, two of the College's professors, James McCosh, professor of logic and metaphysics, and George Dickie, professor of natural history, published *Typical Forms and Special Ends in Creation*, which could be seen as an attempt to bring the Paley-ite world view up to date, including, in the consideration of 'special ends', some allowance for evolutionary ideas. (Though McCosh's biographer W. M. Sloan, is probably exaggerating when he suggests that the book anticipates Darwin.) McCosh, a Free Church of Scotland minister, had been appointed to the post on the strength of his *The Method of Divine Government, Physical and Moral* (1850), which had been recommended by his old fellow-student at Edinburgh, William Gibson. This was an attempt to reconcile Scottish orthodox theology with Scottish philosophy, which, as we have seen, had caused such difficulties for the Belfast Institution in the person of John Ferrie. Like Gibson, McCosh was enthusiastic about the 1859 Revival, and had the revivalist's desire to emphasise the personality of God, rather than simply his identification with the natural or moral law. The conversion of the Synod to a revivalist theology, which required ministers to try to inspire religious experiences among the congregation, was a remarkable if imperceptibly slow development which had occurred within the Synod over the previous twenty years. Although the idea was a feature of the English

James McCosh in 1847 (Ulster Museum).

congregationalist, methodist and baptist traditions, it was new to Scottish presbyterianism.

Gibson, who played an important part in this conversion, had been much influenced by American ideas. In particular, he had the ambition to model Assembly's College on Princeton College, New Jersey, which he described as 'the headquarters of presbyterianism in the world'. There was a distinct American orientation to Ulster presbyterianism at this time. Robert Watts, who arrived in Belfast in 1866, had studied at Princeton and ministered in New York, and in that same year McCosh was appointed president of Princeton, where he was to contend that evolution and natural selection were compatible with Christianity.

He secured this appointment on the strength of a number of books written in Belfast, most notably *An Examination of the Philosophy of John Stuart Mill* (1866). Against Mill's view that the mind can only derive knowledge from its own experience, McCosh argued the old Aristotelian view that the capacity for certain kinds of knowledge is inbuilt in the mind in the form of 'intuitions', a view that harmonises better with the Christian idea of inherited sin. Tyndall, in his Belfast address, touched on the issue and supported this view, adding the interesting qualification, probably derived from Spencer, that such intuitions could be historically evolved and would differ from one society to another.

Generally speaking, however, the presbyterian ministers did not share McCosh's adaptability to the idea of evolution, especially when it was presented in the aggressive form of Tyndall's address. Watts, following Miller, conceded variations within species, but proposed 'a law of maximum variation from the original typical organism' by which the variants would return to type, 'for nothing abnormal can abide long in nature'. Another minister, the Rev. John McNaughtan

William Gibson, founder of the *Banner of Ulster* and chronicler of the Revival (*The Presbyterian College, Belfast 1853–1953* Robert Allen, Belfast, 1954).

(soon to be prominent in a campaign against the stained glass windows in the Assembly's College chapel) said bluntly that 'man, with all his present surroundings, cannot be traced back beyond the 6,000 years exhibited in the Bible chronology'. (He also held that rocks were no proof of antiquity since: 'One act of divine power could surely accomplish in a moment what this conjectural philosophy spreads over 1,000 years'.)

Josias Leslie Porter, five years before he became president of Queen's, argued, in effect, that making hypotheses was an unscientific activity, and that the existence of atoms was unthinkable: 'To conceive of a piece of matter having necessarily, because it is matter,

Josias Leslie Porter, biographer of Henry Cooke and second president of Queen's College, Belfast (*The Presbyterian College, Belfast 1853–1953*, Robert Allen, Belfast, 1954).

length and breadth, and yet being indivisible, is an absurdity.' McCosh himself, who read Tyndall's address on the boat returning to America from a visit to Belfast in 1874, published a reply in which he argued that Darwin's theory was teleological and therefore implied the existence of a super-intelligence: 'In due time, a Paley will arise to furnish proofs of design from such facts as these'.

A more purely scientific response was offered by Joseph John Murphy, son of the founder of the Linfield Mill, and president of the Belfast Natural History and Philosophical Society from 1866–68, and 1871–74. In an address to the Society in 1873 he concentrated his attack not on evolution as such, but on natural selection as the mechanism by which evolution was thought to have occurred. Darwin had argued that variations occur haphazardly then survive and develop because they turn out to be useful. Murphy argued that the odds against a wide range of complementary accidents occurring to produce a complex organ were prohibitive; and that during the period between the appearance of a new characteristic and its evolution into a useful organ, it was more likely to be a hindrance than an aid in the battle for survival. On such grounds he suggested, like McCosh, that if the general idea of evolution was accepted, it would still require a supernatural intelligence directing and overseeing adaptations as they occurred.

It is obviously impossible, in the short space available, to do justice to the intellectual life of a major city in a period of nearly a century, even concentrating, as I have tried to do, on the one aspect of the points at which religious and secular thought interacted. One field—the writing of history—has been completely ignored in this account, though it would include J. S. Reid's important *History of the Presbyterian Church in Ireland*, George Benn's *History of Belfast*, and the appearance of the *Ulster Journal of Archaeology*, together with the entertaining but politically fraught issue of how Belfast viewed the Celtic past.

I hope, however, that I have given some idea of the variety, the typicality and the distinctiveness of thinking in Belfast in this period. I would not like to hazard a generalised reply to the question posed at the beginning of this essay: 'What influence did presbyterianism have on the development of institutions of higher education, and on political, philosophical and scientific thinking in the nineteenth century?' But I think we can suggest that it was less important at the end of the century than it was at the beginning. At the beginning of the century, however liberal their politics or latitudinarian their theology, the presbyterians felt themselves to be a distinct political community with common interests, and they were treated as such by the government. But however much of a problem 'Ulster protestants' might have presented to successive Westminster governments, there was no longer, by the end of the century, a distinctive

Queen's College, Belfast, c. 1861 (Queen's University Library).

presbyterian problem. The main reason for this—as for the decline in the political importance of religion in the rest of the United Kingdom—was probably the decline in the near monopoly the churches had possessed over the dispersal of social and political information. But, among more specific reasons, we may list the development of a secular intellectual centre in Queen's College, Belfast, together with the development of a non-clerical professional intelligentsia, and the separation of theological teaching into a distinct institution of its own; the widespread availability of newspapers as an alternative source of information; the relaxation of the church's control over its people which came about through the Revival and the growth of the gospel hall that followed it; the levelling of relations between the presbyterians and the Church of Ireland that came about through disestablishment; and the increasing difficulty of unquestioning belief in the infallibility and Divine Authorship of the Bible.

9. Community relations and the religious geography 1800–86

Fred Heatley

In the initial decade of the nineteenth century Belfast was relatively small in area with its southern boundary where the City Hall now stands and its northern limits in the vicinity of the present Belfast Co-operative Store's site on Frederick Street. To the west, beyond the Upper Library Street/Millfield line, and the industrialised Divis Street, there were fields and open country, and the River Lagan was nature's boundary to the east. The population, of under 20,000, was located mostly in the heart of the town, in a maze of little entries and alleyways opening off High Street, Hercules Street (now a section of Royal Avenue), Waring Street, Bridge Street, North Street, Donegall Street, Rosemary Lane (now Rosemary Street) and Ann Street. The area to the east of what are now Victoria and Corporation streets was liable to flooding from the waters of Belfast Lough, and the town's principal docks were situated at the bottom of High Street and Waring Street.

Sandy Row was then a huddle of houses beyond the southern limits through which ran, via Malone, the road to Lisburn and Dublin. The Falls, Andersonstown, Shankill, Malone and Stranmillis were rural; and Ballymacarrett (a separate entity from Belfast, to which it was linked by the Long Bridge, built in 1642) was similar, except for a small industrial complex near the Bridge End, and the beginnings of Lagan Village. Ardoyne and the Crumlin Road were still in the future, but while the greatest growth of Belfast was yet to come, the matrix of its industrial base had already been laid.

A cornmill (probably belonging to the Donegalls) had long been in existence in the Millfield/Smithfield area; and with the demand for water power from the recently established cotton industry, and others, a nucleus of factories had sprung up nearby, on the south side of the River Farset, which flowed eastwards from the mountains into the Lagan. There were two reasons for this: the even and relatively predictable flow of the Farset was much more easily controlled than that of its wide-spreading neighbour, the Blackstaff (or indeed the Lagan); and the road to the Falls was a natural extension of High Street, and highly suitable for carting goods to and from the docks.

An 18th century alleyway: Joy's Entry, between High Street and Ann Street 1892 (Ernest Hanford, Ulster Museum).

Yet despite the cotton and linen spinning, the breweries and tanyards, and Ritchie's shipbuilding works, Belfast was principally a centre for the export and import of goods for itself and the surrounding towns and villages. Its location at the head of Belfast Lough, with its safe anchorage for shipping, made it so. The living arrangements of its people were typical of those of any small town of the time. The lower classes had their dwellings in the back streets, or lived in the cellars or garrets of their employers; the middle or business classes resided in or above their shops in the main thoroughfares; and the wealthy had their houses on the town's outskirts. The Donegalls, for example, had their palatial home at Ormeau, and other less distinguished, but notable families had their residences in the unspoilt north of the city, between shore and Cave Hill. The class distinctions were obvious: religious differences were more blurred.

In the days of penal restrictions on catholics Belfast was not the worst place in Ireland for a member of that faith to be. A bastion of protestantism, particularly presbyterianism, since the seventeenth century, it is recorded in 1707 that there were not 'above seven Papists (in the town) and . . . not above 150 Papists in the whole barony'. Yet in reply to an official proclamation for the arrest of the town's catholic clergy, the sovereign of Belfast could report that although Fr Phelomy O'Hamill had been apprehended, he had been offered for his release 'the best Bail the Protestants of this Country affords'. When, during later years, a catholic cutler in Castle Street held occasional mass in his house no action was taken against him, nor was action taken to close premises further along the street in which mass was more regularly said. And when in 1784 the town's first official catholic chapel was opened in Crooked (now Chapel) Lane, there was a subscription from protestants of £84 towards its construction, and the two Belfast Volunteer companies paraded at its opening.

Crooked Lane, later Chapel Lane, showing on left the present St. Mary's church built on the site of the 1784 edifice (Ulster Museum).

In this progressive climate were born the United Irishmen, founded in the town in 1791, a major landmark in Belfast's history. Their espousal of catholic emancipation and the Rights of Man led to the rebellion of 1798, and the imprisonment and hanging of many Belfast protestants. It was a traumatic era for Belfast and its people, and its effects were to linger for a long time in the town.

As a counterweight to Ulster protestant, and especially presbyterian, radicalism, there was the Orange Order which had come into being in 1795, and in spite of disquiet in political and military circles about its activities, leaders such as Lord Castlereagh and general Lake realised its usefulness, and fostered it, turning a blind eye to its campaign against catholics and United Irishmen. But the order was not yet a significant force. The more traditionally minded protestants tended to join the yeomanry corps, which aided the regular troops, and these, in particular the mainly catholic Monaghan Militia, were used in Belfast to quell the activities of the radicals. This all put a severe strain on catholic-protestant relations; and as the new century dawned, and the perturbations roused by Emmet's rebellion of 1803 shook Belfast, it was to be expected that these would suffer intensified pressures. But relationships, as a rule, remained cordial. There were many factors contributing to this and most notable, perhaps, was the catholic acceptance of the Act of Union.

Volunteers parading in High Street, Belfast 14th July 1791 or 1792, from a drawing by John Carey, 1893 (Ulster Museum).

The Act, passed in 1801, was publicly accepted by the spokesmen on the catholic side, though initially opposed by some leading protestants and by several Orange Lodges, who thought it a threat to protestant ascendancy, but when they saw it would confer no extra political rights on catholics it was accepted without further demur. And the catholic condemnation of both the 1798 and 1803 risings also helped to soothe sectarian feelings.

It is worth pausing at this point to consider Belfast's threefold political-religious division, which in general terms might be seen as follows: the members of the established church, the Church of Ireland tended to be Conservative, and probably provided the Orange movement with the bulk of its recruits; the presbyterians as a rule were Liberal, and though there was a tendency towards unity between the protestant churches, many presbyterians regarded the

Church of Ireland establishment with some suspicion. Railing against the 'monstrous union of presbytery and prelacy' in 1835 J. G. Brown, 'John Knox junior', held that 'the proud, lordly, arrogant and insulting establishment' had retarded, rather than advanced the protestant cause. So in many respects then, presbyterians found it easier to identify with the excluded position of catholics. And the catholics, after decades of repression, were only now, by degrees, beginning to assert themselves.

In Belfast, at this time, catholics formed about one-sixth of the populace, and though individual catholic families were to be found scattered throughout the town the vast majority of them were located in the immediate area of the chapel in Crooked Lane, that is, from Hercules Street to Smithfield, one of the poorest district. These catholics held the most menial jobs; and those who were in business on their own were mostly engaged in the victualling trades.

Old Donegall Street, from an engraving by J. Thomson, pub. 1823, showing, from left, late 18th century and early 19th century housing, St. Patrick's presbytery and the original St. Patrick's church (Ulster Museum).

As numbers grew there was need for an additional church, and in 1809 a plot of ground in upper Donegall Street was leased from the marquis of Donegall. St Patrick's church was opened in 1815; and the circumstances of its construction, with protestants subscribing £1,300 of the £4,100 raised to that date, provide an interesting index of the level of community accord. At the consecration its priest, the Rev. William Crolly, expressed 'the gratitude the Catholics felt for the liberality of their Protestant and Dissenting brethren . . . enabling them to erect such a building which could not have been done without their aid'. Hardly surprising, perhaps, when the congregation included the marquis of Donegall, the earls of Londonderry and Massereene, and the town's sovereign and high sheriff, and there were non-catholics acting as collectors. However there is no reason to doubt that the sentiment was genuine and widely felt.

By 1820 Belfast had spread slightly beyond its eighteenth-century limits, mainly along the two roads to Antrim. On one of these, via Shankhill (sic), shops and small businesses had reached Peter's Hill; and on the other, via Millfield, Carrick Hill (now Upper Library Street) and Carrickfergus Street and Road (now North Queen Street), there were new rows of small housing and the town's military barracks. The lower Shankill had been housed almost to Divis Street, the occupants of this development, in Brown's Square, Street and Grove, being mostly weavers and mostly protestant. (As Professor E. Estyn Evans suggests, the above average concentration of presbyterians in the Shankill had much to do with migration from the Scots-settled hinterland of Co. Antrim.) Millfield and Carrick Hill, although also predominantly protestant, had a sprinkling of catholics, although the heaviest concentration remained near the town's centre in the Smithfield/Hercules Street area, now becoming increasingly crowded. In Carrickfergus Street and Road catholics were also well represented; and one notes their increasing prominence in the hotel and drink trades.

Politically, this decade saw an intensification of the fight for the removal of the remaining penal restrictions on catholics, and in Belfast protestant support was much in evidence. Lord Donegall was prepared, as occasion needed, to grant use of the Assembly Rooms for meetings, and speeches in favour of emancipation were given by such eminent local protestants as the Rev. Henry Montgomery of Dunmurry, the McCances and Sinclairs of the upper Falls, Robert Grimshaw, John McAdam, and James Barnett.

There was, of course, opposition from conservatives and the Orange element, and ironically this found voice in the *Belfast News Letter*, once so sympathetic to catholic aims. This did not go unanswered and a new newspaper, the *Northern Whig*, was founded to promote the liberal line. Though Lord Londonderry spoke in parliament against the activities of the Roman Catholic Association, and emancipation's less articulate opponents occasionally threw stones at the windows of the new catholic church, there was generally a welcome for the rights of catholics—offset by a growing fear of their potential political strength. For this reason the passing of the Catholic Relief Act (which brought emancipation) in 1829, was to prove something of a watershed in Belfast's catholic-protestant relations. When Daniel O'Connell, the leading figure in the struggle for catholic demands, turned his attention towards a repeal of the Act of Union, he had little support in protestant Belfast. Initially, however, this did little to inhibit co-operation on less controversial matters such as education and welfare.

The Rev. Dr Crolly, created bishop of Down and Connor in 1825, and the leader of Belfast's catholics, had been active in the non-denominational Lancaster and Brown Street schools; and, though he set up his own denominational Sunday school in St Patrick's after failing to win re-election to the committee which governed these schools, he was well inclined towards the idea of integrated education. He welcomed the non-denominational schooling provided by the National Board of Education, set up in 1831; and

The Rev. Dr Henry Cooke (1788–1868) controversial presbyterian divine and political polemicist. (Frontspiece to *The Life and Times of Henry Cooke, DD, LLD,* by J. L. Porter, London, 1871).

protestants and catholics supported each other in appeals for aid to the Board. The new arrangements, however, quickly met with opposition. In 1832, the Rev. Henry Cooke, who had in 1825 supported the Lancaster and Brown Street schools, which he hoped would 'rub away prejudices', came out firmly against the new system, with an implied attack on the Catholic Church. Crolly defended his position, others took this up, and there were angry exchanges in the newspapers. Crolly continued on his course, and this policy was broadly followed by his successor, Dr Cornelius Denvir. It is notable though, that no other prominent presbyterians took Cooke's blunt stance.

It is difficult to be sure about exactly what led to the swift decay of relations during the 1830s. Certainly it had much to do with the increasing influence of fundamentalist clergymen, led by the formidable Dr Cooke. His presbyterianism was vehemently anti-catholic, and his success in equating home rule with catholicism (and thence the devil) can be judged by the riots which greeted Daniel O'Connell when he visited Belfast in 1841, to speak at a meeting which was attended by many from the more liberal protestant faction, which, interestingly enough, at this time included the Rev. Hugh Hanna. By this date, though still a force, this group was firmly in retreat.

Another unhelpful factor was rural immigration, which, from the twenties to the middle of the century was mainly catholic. Not only did this affect the religious balance (by 1850 catholics formed one-third of the population), to the disquiet of some protestants, but,

A cartoon illustrating Daniel O'Connell's visit to Belfast, 1841 (*The Repealer Repulsed*, Ulster Museum). In centre is the old White Linen Hall and at right Kern's Hotel where 'The Liberator' stayed.

more importantly, it pressed the town's resources, and increased the competition for jobs and living accommodation. Many of the newcomers failed to find work, and the widespread practice of keeping jobs for one's co-religionists acted greatly to their disadvantage. Indeed in 1842 conditions were so bad that the distressed besieged the workhouse begging for food, and a few days later the military were called upon to disperse a crowd which had gathered outside Bernard Hughes' bakery, pleading for bread. The military were so horrified that they subscribed £20 to a fund established to assist the hungry. While this poverty was in part attributable to slump, a government commission of inquiry laid much of the blame at the door of the town fathers, it noted:

> The Corporation, as now conducted, embraces no principle of representation and confers on the inhabitants no benefit. No power of control or check is preserved: the proceedings are carried on without publicity and the consequences have been . . . great neglect and abuse of trusts . . .'

The distress was augmented as the decade neared its close and the effects of the Famine were felt throughout Ireland. The potato blight struck heaviest in Connacht and Munster, and although Ulster was much less devastated it was in the strongly catholic counties of Cavan and Monaghan, and in parts of Tyrone and Armagh, that its depredations were most keenly felt. Many of the small farmers and their families had to flee the land and for them Belfast, as Ireland's most industrialised town, offered the best prospects for survival. Their route lay down the Lurgan corridor into Lisburn and the western and southern approaches to Belfast, where the mills and other industries in the lower Falls must have been a prime attraction, and it is from this period that we find the area becoming preponderantly catholic. As has been mentioned, this increased tensions, and sectarian rioting, which had first occurred during the 1832 elections, became a recurring feature of life in the town. Serious disturbances occurred in 1845, 1857 and 1863, especially in the area between the protestant Sandy Row and the catholic Pound, where disturbances were almost commonplace. (According to the police inquiry into the 1857 disturbances, the 'Pound', designated as the area within Barrack Street, Durham Street, Divis Street, the Falls Road and Albert Street, was by then exclusively catholic).

The people of the 'Pound' celebrate the centenary of the 1798 rebellion (Ulster Museum).

In 1851 the bulk of the population of over 100,000 were settled in religiously segregated quarters. Smithfield and Hercules Street were still the main catholic centres, and the fact that members of the Young Ireland Party, a militant breakaway from O'Connell's grouping, sought refuge and found some measure of support there when planned talks were opposed by equally militant protestants, may point to the sentiment of the districts at the time. Another catholic quarter was at the back of York Street, running into Waring Street and Corporation Street. (The appalling conditions here were brought to public notice by the Rev. W. M. O'Hanlon of Donegall Street congregationalist church in a series of powerful letters to the *Northern Whig.*)

Protestantism was in greatest strength in Sandy Row, the Shankill and the Falls, where the mill owners in the lower sector of the district were all protestants, as were the farmers and mill owners in the middle Falls and Andersonstown. This strength in the Falls is evidenced by the constant building of protestant places of worship on, or close to, Divis Street and the Falls Road, beginning with Christ church in College Square North in 1833. By the end of the century, between Divis Street and Suffolk there were six churches belonging to the Church of Ireland, seven to the presbyterians and two to the methodists, with Broadway Presbyterian being built as late as 1896. In contrast, there was no catholic church on the Falls until St Peter's was opened in 1866, followed by the erection of a temporary chapel by the Redemptorist Fathers at Clonard in 1897, and the building of St Paul's, just above Springfield Road, also in the last years of the century.

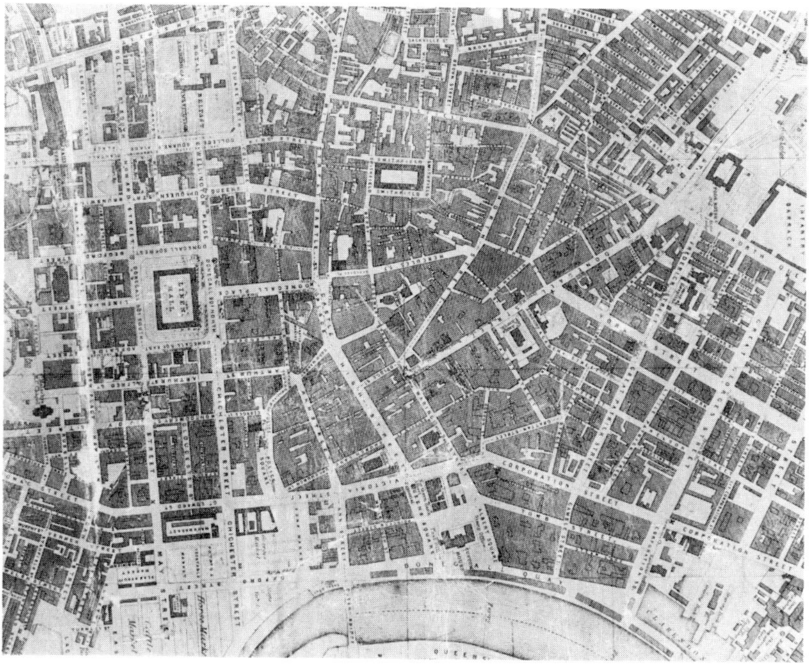

Section from 1870 map of Belfast.

By 1850 there had been a great growth in housing and industry. Ballymacarrett had expanded and was to be linked to Belfast proper by two new bridges, and shipbuilding was shortly to be transferred to this side of the River Lagan, as Dargan's Island became Queen's Island and was converted to industrial purposes. A temporary catholic chapel had been opened in Ballymacarrett in 1831 but the area remained predominantly protestant.

Meanwhile at Cromac, in what became the 'Upper Markets', large town residences along the lines of Dublin's Georgian terraces had been built for the commercial gentry. They had the advantage of being convenient to the business sector at an upkeep which was not excessive. But the development of the 'Malone Ridge' during the 1850s and 1860s drew many of the more affluent away from the district, a process accelerated by the construction of a large linen-finishing complex with its associated firms to the rear of the White Linen Hall. Fortunately, unlike Dublin where many of the larger town residences were purchased by speculators and turned into cheap tenement blocks, the houses in the Henrietta Street district of

Poverty in the back streets. Raphael Street in the 'Lower Markets' (Welch Collection, Ulster Museum).

Belfast were not quite big enough to be successfully sub-divided. Some were made into temporary lodging houses and only relatively recently have they begun to be demolished.

The area began to pass into catholic hands, and acquired a chapel in 1844, though at that period the bulk of its congregation must either have come from outside the district, or have been engaged in service to the local gentry. St Malachy's, one of the most elegant of Belfast's churches, was, it is believed, intended to be the town's catholic cathedral. (This plan never came to fruition, but it is worth noting the free grant of one-fifth of the original site, by a protestant, Adam McClean.) In time the 'Upper Markets' became almost exclusively catholic, and a nunnery and catholic schools were established. The 'Lower Markets', a much humbler location on the opposite side of Cromac Street, also became a catholic enclave.

Bishop Denvir was to remain leader of Belfast's catholics until the mid-1860s, but his latter years were not happy ones, dogged by schisms amongst the laity, while on the streets protestants and catholics engaged in often bloody battles. A liberal and humble man in religious and social matters he sought to stay on amicable terms with his neighbours. But moderation was no longer the fashion, a militant faction was in the ascendant, and there were fierce debates within the Roman Catholic Church on such issues as segregated education, and the role of the laity in church affairs. Matters came to a head in 1850 with the appointment of the apostolic delegate, Dr Paul Cullen, as archbishop of Armagh, in succession to archbishop William Crolly. Cullen had a specific mandate from Rome to unify the church in Ireland, and at the Thurles Synod, in August 1850, he managed to have the Queen's Colleges (in Belfast, Cork and Galway) deemed unsuitable for catholic students. This, and other matters, were seen in Belfast as 'Papal aggression'.

Denvir had other problems. The observation in 1863, by the archbishop of Armagh, archbishop Dixon, that only one in three Belfast catholics attended Sunday Mass may have been an exaggeration, but attendances at this time were far from satisfactory. (This, together with lack of money, may account for the absence of catholic churches on the Falls.) Of equal concern was the problem of illiteracy, the 1861 census returns show that in Belfast 30.2 per cent

A Twelfth of July Orange procession passing through Shaftsbury Square in the 1890s (Welch Collection, Ulster Museum). This area has changed much since then.

of catholics were illiterate, against 10.2 per cent of protestants. Though unable to tackle poverty, the underlying cause, bishop Denvir brought the Sisters of Mercy to the town, and his successor, bishop Dorrian, invited the Christian Brothers, two orders recognised for their teaching abilities. Their introduction, plus a multitude of schools managed by catholic laity, did much to improve matters, and a certain amount to break the vicious circle of lack of education, leading to poorly paid work, and continued impoverishment.

The upswing in trade occasioned by the American Civil War in the 1860s provided more employment, and led to the working class development of north Belfast and the Crumlin Road, but it did little to alleviate street disorder. What it did do though was to give final character to the Shankill Road, which, sandwiched between two highly industrialised thoroughfares, and having no industry of its own, became the shopping centre for the Falls and Crumlin roads, and supplied workers to the mills on each. It also became the home of protestant opposition to home rule, though ironically one of its most famous sons, the Rev. Isaac Nelson (c. 1812–88) retired from the presbyterian ministry to succeed Charles Stewart Parnell as nationalist MP for Co. Mayo in the 1880s. (Nelson's residence was 'Sugarfield House', from which Sugarfield Street takes its name, and it was to him that the Nelson Memorial church was dedicated.)

The demolition of Hercules Street in 1879. Note how narrow the old throughfare was (Ulster Museum).

The demolition, in the 1870s, of the old, unhygienic Hercules Street to make way for the wider and more modern Royal Avenue added another piece of loyalty to Belfast street nomenclature and brought about the dispersal of the area's inhabitants. Some of them moved into Smithfield, others to Millfield and more, perhaps, to the lower Falls creating, by the end of the century, a strong line of catholicism reaching from the Pound, through Millfield and Carrick

Hill, to North Queen Street. Pockets of catholics were also to be found in the Short Strand area of Ballymacarrett, in the immediate vicinity of the docks off Garmoyle Street, and on the Shore Road; but from the 1870s the expansion of catholic areas was not equal to that of protestant districts, for the immigration of these years was predominantly protestant and there was a certain amount of catholic emigration, indeed in 1901 catholics accounted for only 24 per cent of the population.

However as early as the 1860s community separateness was almost complete. The drama of British parliamentarianism was played out in physical violence on the streets of Belfast. Gladstone's Home Rule Bill of 1886 split the local Liberals, most of whom, including the extremely wealthy Belfast catholic Arthur Hamill,

Belfast riots of 1886 (Welch Collection, Ulster Museum). 'Bower's Hill Barracks' on the Shankill Road the morning after being attacked by unionists protesting against home rule.

rushed to become Ulster unionists. The divisions became more straightforward, and the Presbyterian Church fell into alliance with the Church of Ireland as protestantism became identified with unionism and catholicism with nationalism. Though unifying causes were thin on the ground, there were brief rapprochements: in 1874, catholic and protestant millworkers had briefly united in a six week struggle to prevent a 10 per cent cut in their wages, but such bright spots were few. The divisions were symbolically embodied two years afterwards, when the statue of the liberal and popular young earl of Belfast was removed to make way for a statue of the hero of the Orange faction, Dr Cooke. By the time of the Home Rule Bill community relations had more or less assumed what was to become their twentieth-century form. Then as now the voluble and the extremists were the moving agents, the dictators of events, and their sayings and deeds are forever in type; the voices and actions of the moderate are much more difficult to find.

10. Politics and the rise of the skilled working man

Paul Bew

> According to all Socialist theories North East Ulster being the most developed industrially, ought to be the quarter in which class lines of cleavage, politically and industrially should be the most pronounced, the class rebellion the most common. As a cold matter of fact it is the happy hunting ground of the slave driver and the home of the least rebellious slaves in the industrial world.
>
> James Connolly, Irish socialist

> Belfast was, he thought, an elysium for working men. In Belfast they had large steel and iron shipbuilding yards where fathers and sons could be employed. They also had what was termed their staple industry, the linen industry, where the wives and daughters found employment (Applause). If there was not sufficient employment in these places they had the largest rope manufacturing establishment in the world (Hear, Hear).
>
> James Henderson, lord mayor of Belfast

The period from 1860 to 1870 was the key decade in Belfast's industrial and demographic growth. The population rose by more than 40 per cent—from 121,602 to 174,412, the largest increase since 1800. The cotton famine, a product of the American Civil War, allowed linen to enter markets hitherto the preserve of cotton. The linen industry, the largest employer in the city, with a largely female labour force, was however almost completely ununionised.

In contrast to linen, shipbuilding and engineering had a labour force with large groups of workers in jobs which had a relatively high level of trade union organisation throughout the United Kingdom. Metal workers had been unionised in Belfast since the first half of the century—the Iron Moulders had a branch from 1826, the Boilermakers from 1841, and when the Amalgamated Society of Engineers was established in 1851, there were already branches of its constituent unions in Belfast.

This group of workers was characterised by an intense sectionalism. They were obsessively concerned with the protection of their place in the labour market and the work process. Inevitably therefore, there were regular disputes with other workers, skilled and unskilled. Whereas in linen there were only a minority of workers, adult males, who earned wages of over £1 per week at the end of the century, shipbuilding and engineering employed large numbers of skilled and relatively well paid workers. In the 1880s skilled workers in Belfast engineering plants were making rates comparable to the national average, whilst Belfast labourers were on a much lower rate. In 1910 the fitter's rate in Belfast was exceeded only by rates in London, South Wales and Sheffield, and in general the rates of skilled workers in shipbuilding, engineering and building were closely comparable with those in the main centres of the United Kingdom.

A word of caution may be necessary here. These undoubted facts have led many to speculate that the existence of an aristocracy of labour 'explains' the strength of Orangeism within the Belfast working class. This argument is, however, not a strong one. It is certainly clear that catholics were under-represented in skilled occupations throughout the nineteenth century. However, it is also clear that the majority of unskilled workers were protestants and their politics were often intensely sectarian. It seems impossible to explain their views by references to any 'privilege'. None of this, of course, takes away from the fact that the unionised groups formed Belfast's artisan and largely protestant working class elite.

1860–70 was the decade in which this group, armed with the vote by the 1867 Reform Act, began to have a very significant effect on the city's politics. While in the late sixties the more upper-crust Conservatives and Orangemen were concerned about the threat to the established position of the Church of Ireland, urban and

Daniel O'Connell

A prohibited meeting of the Land League at Brookeborough, Co. Fermanagh (*Illustrated London News*, December 1880).

working class Orangemen were nonplussed by the whole question. For them the key issue was the government's restrictions on protestant rights of marching—exemplified by the recent Party Processions legislation.

'Indomitable' William Johnston of Ballykilbeg emerged as their champion. Having arranged to get himself jailed for a month by illegal marching, Johnston sought popularity as an Orange martyr. The author of anti-catholic novels, Johnston posed as a champion both of working class and Orange interests. He formed an alliance—to get financial support—with the city's beleaguered liberal bourgeois elite. In 1868 he inflicted a significant blow on the town's Conservative machine by topping the Belfast poll in the general election of that year. But Johnston was in severe financial trouble and was easily bought off by a relatively minor offer of government patronage in 1878. The letter in which Sir Thomas Bateson, MP for Devizes, and a significant figure in Belfast tory circles, canvassed Johnston's claims to Benjamin Disraeli still survives and is of some interest:

> The man certainly has claims on our party. He could have played the very devil with us in Ireland. He was and still is a great power with the masses of Orangemen and had he been so minded he might have carried many of them over to the enemy . . . If he is now provided with a comfortable colonial appointment he will in return furnish the government with a seat for Mr May your present law adviser. Nothing would gratify the great bulk of the working men of Belfast more than to see their idol, Ballykilbeg, comfortably provided for. They would almost take it as a compliment to themselves . . .

Within a remarkably short period Johnston then reached an accommodation with the local tory machine and was re-integrated within Conservative politics. But the significance of the episode lies not just in the matter of his personal destiny, for the whole affair also reveals that the Belfast Conservative organisation now had to pay attention to a new social force—the Belfast working man. The 'Johnston of Ballykilbeg' affair represented the birth of a populist Orangeism—pro-working class, democratic and sectarian in tone—which was to play a major role in the evolution of the city's politics. Typical exemplars of this approach were E. S. W. de Cobain, MP for East Belfast (1885–1892) and Thomas Sloan, MP for South Belfast (1902–10). The strength of this tradition made the work of Belfast's non-sectarian socialists and democrats very hard.

The 1900s, however, opened up new and relatively benign possibilities for the development of the city's progressive forces. In the late 1890s and early 1900s home rule for Ireland appeared to lose much of its appeal for the leadership of the British Liberal party; and with the Conservatives already solidly opposed to Irish nationalism, Belfast was able to slip into a more relaxed mood. The difficult years of 1886 and 1893, when home rule had appeared to be just around the corner, now seemed to belong to a bad dream.

Also important was the fact that, especially after the summer of 1902, 'moderate' tendencies began to gain strength within Irish nationalism. In particular, William O'Brien MP, who had founded the United Irish League in 1898 and was a leader of the front rank, became a convert to the doctrine of conciliation of the Irish Unionist minority. Even before O'Brien's 'conversion', the United Irish League had co-operated with T. W. Russell's land reform movement among the Ulster tenantry.

In 1886 and 1893 both O'Brien, as a nationalist, and T. W. Russell (MP for Tyrone South), as a unionist, had been bitter opponents.

National Rent Office at Loughrea, after the arrest of Messrs O'Brien and Dillon (*Illustrated London News*, January 1887).

However, their common participation in the land reform movement—followed by the largely successful conference discussions with landlords and government which culminated in the Land Purchase Act of 1903—inclined both men towards the view that a new era was opening up in Irish politics. As much of the protestant landed ascendancy seemed prepared to retire gracefully from their dominant position, many of the old sectarian catch-cries of Irish politics seemed to be losing their relevance. O'Brien did not cease to be a nationalist and nor, for the moment, did Russell cease to be a unionist, but they both argued that Irishmen on both sides of the political and religious divide should do everything in their power to generate an atmosphere of toleration and patriotism.

In the autumn of 1903, Russell published an article in O'Brien's paper the *Irish People* which expressed this mood perfectly. 'I am a double dyed Unionist,' he wrote, 'I am for a Union of the Irish people as well as Union with the people of Great Britain.' Addressing the home rulers he wrote:

> What ought Nationalists to do? My answer is plain. It ought to be the duty of every Nationalist and every man belonging to the majority of the Irish people to make it easy for the minority of his fellow countrymen to do the right by Ireland—make it hard for them to do the wrong . . . Let them repress sectarian strife as if it were the plague.

Then he spoke to the unionists:

> It is not our duty to obstruct National sentiment. Our duty lies in the opposite direction. It is our duty diligently to seek out opportunities for hearty co-operation with our Nationalist fellow countrymen; to vie with them in our desire to work for the regeneration of the country.

Russell repudiated vulgar Ulster chauvinism: 'I do not share the thoughtless and ignorant view, so common in the Northern land, that Ulster is Ireland—that nothing else counts'; and stressed the unifying effect of the recent land agitation: 'In presbyterian Down and Antrim and in Orange Fermanagh many of the Unionist farmers have gone to the poll with their Nationalist fellow countrymen—have rejected all attempts to confuse the issue and have to a large extent put behind their backs the sectarian cries of the past'. Beneath the surface there were further positive developments which newspapers failed to appreciate. The younger generation of presbyterian ministers were solidly in favour of concessions to catholics on higher educational matters and the presbyterian clergy as a whole only narrowly opposed. Then Russell broached the heart of the matter:

> Another matter I approach with much greater difficulty. I mean the evolution of the democratic Orangeman. I never belonged to the Orange Society—and I know nothing of its inner working. But its public history is open to everybody. And the thing borne in upon one's mind in connection with it is that this powerful and organised body of men has been patronised and used by the landlords for the maintenance of

landlordism. Whatever may have been its primary objects—this is the base use to which they have been put. But the Ulster land movement has settled this as well as other things. In Antrim there were Orange districts which voted solidly with the Nationalists for Land Reform. In Fermanagh—the home of the Imperial Grand Master—the same thing took place. But the real revolt has taken place in Belfast. There is no need to enter into particulars. What it all means is that the scales have fallen from the eyes of some of the people—that the democratic instincts of the Belfast artisan have revolted against the autocratic tutelage to which he has been so long subject. *For, strange as it may appear, the Belfast artisan is not a Tory. He is a Radical with a monomania about the Pope which colours his whole life and bedevils his every action.* At present they are as men escaping from a dark room into the sunlight. They are dazed and hardly know where they are. But with capable leaders and with a little more intercourse with their fellow-countrymen, and with the artisans of England they will see things as they really are. To sum up—the situation places, in my opinion, *a very heavy responsibility* upon all those who lead or who influence in any way the public opinion of the country.

Russell's remarks here are clearly alluding—though they do not mention the organisation specifically—to the newly formed Independent Orange Order which had been founded in 1903. The IOO leaders made the air thick with apparently radical denunciations of 'landlordism' and 'capitalism'. The IOO's famous Magheramorne manifesto, published in July 1905, has been seen by some historians as an expression of a genuine liberal patriotism. Russell was writing as a leader who shared an ambit with the IOO—he had stood on a common platform with many of its leaders. He also enjoyed a

Keir Hardie addressing a North Belfast election meeting on behalf of William Walker, 1906 (Ulster Museum). Walker is the seated figure at the right of the picture.

position of importance within unionism, and in spite of his 'liberal' pronouncements, his prestige as a land reformer was such that it was official policy for unionists not to attack him—much to the disgust of some Conservatives.

The Independent Order had reasonable support. A sober estimate would suggest the Order had a membership in Belfast of about one thousand at its high point in 1905—the official Order having perhaps eight to nine thousand members. While this new movement was obviously, therefore, substantially smaller than the old Order, it was nonetheless of significance, and had very capable leaders in Thomas Sloan MP, and its Grand Master, Lindsay Crawford. But how accurate was Russell's estimate of the IOO's politics? Were they really breaking with sectarianism 'as men escaping from a dark room into sunlight'? In fact, the Independent Orange Order represented—in an admittedly more sophisticated form—another variant of that populist and sectarian democratic Orange politics which had first surfaced in the days of Billy Johnston of Ballykilbeg.

In the early 1900s the Ulster unionist MPs at Westminster had become increasingly integrated within British toryism. In the same period, the British Conservative government adopted a generally conciliatory stance towards the Catholic Church in Ireland. In this context, it was easy enough to portray the Ulster MPs as insufficiently vigorous defenders of protestantism. The scene was set for populist challenges from men such as Sloan. Even Lindsay Crawford, the most advanced and most 'intellectual' of the IOO leaders was capable of brutally insisting that:

> the working men of Belfast are Protestant and they place their Protestantism before party politics, they look for the protection of their interest to the representatives not of Labour minus Protestantism but to the Protestant Democracy which embraces Labour.

Nevertheless, it was perhaps inevitable that nationalists would 'misread' the significance of the new anti-tory mood in Belfast working class politics. In February 1906 John Redmond, the leader of the Irish Parliamentary Party, declared:

> The most hopeful sign in the Ireland of today is the change that is rapidly coming over the opinions and sentiments of the people of Ulster and of Belfast . . . We have waited all these years, mistakes have been made upon our side as well as upon the other, and those of us who believe in Ireland a Nation have been waiting all these years for the dawn of the day when Protestant Orange working men in the North of Ireland would begin to understand that, after all, Ireland a Nation means as much for them as for us—freedom, prosperity and happiness—and how many of our race, how many of our comrades and friends in the last 25 years have gone down to the grave in despair of ever seeing that day. But the day has dawned.

By 1907–8 the new mood apparently detected in such comments no longer existed. The official Conservative leadership had to a

Illustration which accompanied 'Hope for the Future', T. W. Russell's article in the *Irish People* (Vol. 5, no. 216).

significant degree 'reformed itself', and by adopting a more critical attitude towards British tory conciliation of Irish clericalism, prevented any further development of populist Orange politics in the city. Secondly, far from nationalists having taken T. W. Russell's advice to 'suppress sectarian strife as if it were the plague', the reverse had happened. Specifically anti-protestant forces such as the Ancient Order of Hibernians had gained a much greater hold on Irish nationalism than ever before. As William O'Brien's dissident nationalist paper the *Irish People* noted on 27 April 1907, 'moderate' candidates were losing ground in Belfast. It pointed out the electoral fate of Labour's William Walker; who had previously polled well:

> The North Belfast election is a proof that the Unionist campaign which has been carried on in Ulster is producing the results which were expected from it. Mr Clark's majority was 1,827 as compared with 291 for the late Sir D. Dixon who was believed to have been the strongest candidate that could have been put forward. The Unionist poll showed an increase of over 1,100 votes, while there was a falling off of 420 in the votes recorded for Mr Walker as compared with the General Election. There is no use in hiding from ourselves that these are ugly facts. Even though Mr Walker did not stand as a Liberal or as a Home Ruler, a victory for him would have enormously strengthened the position of the Government as showing that the power of the official Unionist gang was broken in Belfast. Now Unionists can boast that they have actually strengthened their position . . . . The Ulster Guardian, which was the only paper that supported Mr Walker, among other contributory causes, attributes the reduction of his poll to the defection of old Orange Trades Unionists.

Matters deteriorated further when, from 1910 onwards, home rule again appeared to be a reasonably serious political prospect. By the time the greatest figure in the history of Irish socialism, James Connolly, arrived in Belfast to begin his work as a labour organiser, Belfast had returned to its old ways. In July 1913 Connolly bitterly wrote to a friend: 'The feeling of the city is so violently Orange and anti-Home Rule at present that our Task has been a hard one all along'.

In this very different context, Connolly had perhaps understandably no sympathy for the sentimental illusions of a John Redmond. This comes out clearly in his famous Belfast debate with William Walker. When Walker, a Labour man much in the style of the Magheramorne manifesto, but unlike Connolly not a nationalist, reminded Connolly of the contribution made by protestants to the cause of Irish democracy, Connolly caustically replied:

> We do not care so much what a few men did, as what the vast mass of their co-religionists do. The vast mass of the Protestants of Ulster except during the period of 1798 were the bitter enemies of the men he has named and during the bitter struggle of the Land League, the sturdy Protestant democracy of the North were electing landlords and the nominees of landlords to every Protestant constituency in Ulster.

As a matter of historical fact, he is quite wrong on this score. The epoch of the Land League (1879–82) saw a vigorous revival of agrarian radicalism in *both* the catholic and protestant tenant farming communities. 'Landlords' and 'the nominees of landlords'

Moonlighters cutting the telegraph wires (*Illustrated London News*, March 1887), Land league activity united protestant and catholic.

found life at the polls very hard indeed; and it took the massive miscalculation of the so-called nationalist invasion of Ulster in 1883-4 to put the tories back in the driving seat in rural Ulster. Connolly's remarks illustrate an astonishing ignorance of the progressive traditions of rural Ulster—especially surprising as these had re-surfaced in T. W. Russell's movement of the early 1900s.

Redmond had seen an upsurge in democratic struggle within the protestant community as indicating a move towards nationalism. Connolly, on the other hand, finding no sympathy for nationalism, had gone on to presume the absence of democratic traditions. Both failed to confront the fundamental source of unionist strength; the contrast that could so easily be made between an expansionist industrial capitalism in Belfast, and southern under-development. This was why the Belfast lord mayor, Sir James Henderson, could tell the delegates to the 1898 Irish TUC conference in Belfast that the city was an 'elysium for working men' and be applauded and not hooted. Politically perhaps it may have been impossible for a Redmond or a Connolly to face this fact and its implications.

11. The city and the country

Leslie Clarkson

'Belfast, a sea-port, borough, market town, and parish . . .'

Thus wrote Samuel Lewis in his *Topographical Dictionary of Ireland* published in 1837. These were the foundations on which the development of Belfast in the eighteenth century rested and which continued to support its evolution as Ireland's only major industrial city in the nineteenth century. They bound town and country together in a close relationship. As a sea-port Belfast carried the produce of the Ulster countryside to the wider world beyond and brought back, in return, raw materials and consumer goods demanded by the inhabitants of the city and its hinterland. As a borough, Belfast extended the functions of government, administration and culture over a wide area. As a market town, it witnessed the busy comings and goings of city and country dwellers meeting together to buy and sell. And as a parish it exercised religious and secular influence far into counties Antrim, Down and beyond. No successful city exists in isolation from its rural surroundings. Belfast was no exception and in its case the close ties between town and country were epitomised by its physical setting, which confined the built-up area within a rim of hills and afforded even the meanest brick-red street a glimpse of green.

The strongest links between Belfast and the countryside were provided by her people. In 1800 the city contained roughly 20,000 people, in 1841, 75,000, and in 1901, 349,000. The population grew by 3 per cent per annum during the nineteenth century. Such a rate could not be achieved merely by an excess of births over deaths no matter how lusty its young men and women and however healthy the environment—the city was, in fact, extremely unhealthy—but depended on a continuous influx of people from the countryside. In the 1850s and '60s alone almost 90,000 people were added to the city's population as men and women came from the shattered post-Famine countryside to work in the rapidly expanding textile factories, engineering works and shipyards. In the last three decades of the century the pace slightly slackened but even so the population of Belfast doubled. The result was that in 1901 only one-fifth of householders living in the city had been born in Belfast. One half came from counties Antrim and Down, beyond the city boundaries, and the remaining 30 per cent from elsewhere in Ireland, Britain, or

View of Belfast, 1793 (John Nixon, Ulster Museum). At the end of the 18th century Belfast was still a small country town of fewer than 20,000 people. This idealized view gives a strong impression of the countryside pressing close to the city.

abroad. (One presumes that the 26 Chinamen living in Belfast in 1901 were sailors or laundrymen, but there are no obvious explanations of why the solitary Arab and the lone Mexican had strayed so far from home.) Admittedly the bulk of the children of householders were Belfast born; however none of the migration statistics suggest that Belfast was a cosmopolitan community.

Most of the thousands who came to Belfast are anonymous men and women, mere numbers in census columns, but a few are known to us through their achievements. For example, James Thomson arrived from Ballynahinch in 1816 to be professor of mathematics at the newly established Academical Institution. He built a house in College Square East where later his more illustrious son, the future Lord Kelvin, was born. Roughly thirty years later the family of William James Pirrie, the driving force behind Harland and Wolff, settled in Belfast from Little Clandeboye in County Down—the Pirries came the long way round, via Quebec. Another shipyard immigrant was A. M. Carlisle, Pirrie's general manager, and 'the greatest shipyard manager in Europe'. Born in Ballymena in 1854, he was brought to Belfast by his parents in 1816 when his father was appointed headmaster of the English department at the Academical Institution. A few years before the elder Carlisle had been appointed to Inst., the Presbyterian Church set up its own College. All but one of the foundation professors were Ulster, not Belfast, born—the sole exception coming from Scotland.

These men, and others like them, made major contributions to the community and intellectual life of Belfast, but by sheer weight of numbers they were surpassed by the masses who were neither leaders of industry nor educationalists, but toiled untutored in the city's factories and workshops. Only occasionally do we catch a

Nos. 12–14 College Square East, c. 1880 (Welch Collection Ulster Museum). Birth place of Lord Kelvin. The terrace was built in the early 19th century to house the city's professional classes, but when the photograph was taken it was already becoming converted to commercial uses. Note the gas lamps and tram lines.

glimpse of them. There was, for example, the father of the distinguished Belfast-born historian, T. W. Moody, a shipyard worker from County Londonderry, whose own father was 'an unskilled worker who could give his only child no more than an elementary education'. For such people Belfast offered the prospect of moving up the occupational and educational ladder, as well as providing higher earnings than could be obtained in the countryside. Most migrants, though, arrived without skills and remained so, exchanging the labouring jobs of the countryside for those of the city.

For women, particularly, work in Belfast promised a modicum of economic and social independence. Nineteenth-century Belfast offered more opportunities for women's work than many British cities, especially from the mid-century with the rapid expansion of the linen industry. As a result there were substantially more women in Belfast than men. In 1841 there were 38,000 females and 32,000 males; in 1901 the ratio was 188,000 to 162,000. The imbalance was particularly marked in the case of young immigrants, aged 15–24, among whom there were 100 females for every 71 males (among young catholics the ratio was 100:58). Women clustered especially in the linen industry, which in 1901 employed 24,000 females but only 7,000 males. Women were also found in large numbers in the clothing trades (11,000 compared to 4,000 males), and in domestic service, which employed almost 8,000 women and girls and provided 13 per cent of all female employment. We may not think the life of a mill girl was a particularly attractive one. One observer in the early part of this century wrote that Belfast's 'main trade, linen spinning and weaving, does not appeal to the imagination; the

View of Belfast c. 1850 (after Andrew Nicholl, Ulster Museum). Although Belfast's population had increased almost five-fold since the late 18th century, the view looking across to Cave Hill shows that Belfast still possessed a strongly rural character. The ships clustered in the habour just beyond the bridge and the smoking chimneys, however, an indicative of the growing importance of commerce and industry.

factories are great hives of shut-up operatives, mainly women, and not over highly paid'. But compared to the restrictive, male-dominated environment of the family farm, it offered both financial independence and the chance of marrying a man of one's choice. In the words of the 'Doffers Song', describing the lives of the girls who 'doffed' the bobbins from the spinning machines:

> You will easy know a doffer
> When she comes into town,
> With her long yeller hair,
> And her ringlets hanging down
>
> You will always know a doffer,
> For she'll always get her man.

Belfast's rural migrants spun an intricate web of kinship, binding together town and country. In one direction country girls obtained jobs in the spinning mills by being 'spoken for' by relatives already in employment. City relatives, too, were useful staging-posts for newcomers from the country, and nearly a quarter of all Belfast households in 1901 contained related kin other than children—brothers and sisters, uncles, cousins and the like. In return, country cousins in counties Down or Antrim were the focus of the occasional day out, or the source of gifts of eggs or butter and perhaps a chicken at Christmas.

The census of 1841 vividly reveals the extent of city–country intercourse. In that year Belfast contained 2,700 people 'ministering to food', including 1,000 farmers, graziers, ploughmen and gardeners. The group also included 221 bakers and a score of millers and flour

The Lagan at New Forge, c. 1884 (Welch Collection, Ulster Museum). The Lagan was vitally important to the development of Belfast. It linked the city to its rich hinterland in south and central Ulster, provided power for its early industry and a site for its harbour and shipyards. It also gave the citizens of Belfast easily accessible country walks.

dealers. Among them was Bernard Hughes, baker and flour merchant, with premises in Lancaster Street (off York Street), but soon to expand to Donegall Place, Donegall Street, and the Falls Road. His business illustrates in miniature the links between town and country. In 1852 Hughes baked between 500 and 600 bags of flour a week, modestly promising 'the inhabitants of Belfast and vicinity', that he could provide bread 'manufactured, pure and unadulterated, as cheap or cheaper, than any part of the United Kingdom, or even the world'. In two days before Christmas, 1851, he made '126 Batches and 60 ovensfull of Small Bread, consuming 710 cwts of Flour . . .' producing bread worth £482. Such an output—perhaps 60,000 loaves—was beyond the capacity of Belfast families to consume by themselves, even at Christmas. As well as bread, Hughes offered for sale 'Carlow Oatmeal', 'Patent Oatmeal, coarse and fine, manufactured by Wm Langtry and Co., Portadown, and Patent Exhibition Oatmeal by McCann and Co. Drogheda'. We do not know the extent of Hughes' bread sales, but at the end of the century another Belfast bakery, the OPB (Old Public Bakery) dispatched its bread carts daily to Doagh and the surrounding countryside where its loaves and buns were bought by local families as a treat and a change from home baking.

Also 'ministering to food' were 166 butchers, many of whom lived in Hercules Street (where Royal Avenue now runs) which functioned as a daily street market thronged with 'farmers and fisherfolk, merchants and pedlars, huxters, egg-wives and waggoners . . .' Other butchers were found in Smithfield where 'country people gathered, wide-eyed among the rolls of gaudy woven stuff with which the barrows were piled high'. There were far too many butchers in Belfast for the supply of the city alone and many of their customers lived in the surrounding towns and villages. Some of the hides that were by-products of the butchers' trade went into the manufacture of leather which was used, in turn, by the city's 1,195 shoemakers. At this point in the nineteenth century, boot and shoemaking was still mainly a localized craft and Belfast boot makers satisfied a demand within the city and the immediately surrounding countryside, but no further afield.

During the early decades of the nineteenth century Belfast developed as a major coaching town. The route between the city and Dublin had long been important, but with the growth of Belfast as a port and manufacturing centre, and with the industrial development

Castle Place 1843. Throughout the 19th century Castle Place was the centre of the city and terminus of the coaching services. The illustration shows a stage coach outside the Donegall Arms Hotel.

of the Lagan valley, Belfast became the terminus of services extending south-westwards to Armagh, Monaghan, Dungannon, Enniskillen and Sligo. In 1841 there were more than 300 coach and car drivers, carriers and cabmen in the town, as well as 73 hotel and innkeepers and 312 tavern keepers catering for the needs of travellers and visitors. The coaches departed from prominent hotels in the city. In the early nineteenth century, for example, the Derry coach set off daily from the Donegall Arms in Castle Place at 11.30 a.m., to arrive in Derry at 4 a.m. the following morning. There were two coaches a day to Dublin leaving from Castle Place in the centre of the city. One left at 4 p.m. and journeyed throughout the night and following day to reach Dublin at 7 in the evening; the other departed at 5 a.m., arriving at 7 a.m. the following morning. By the mid-century the journey had been reduced to twelve hours. The traditional route southward from the city was via Castle Street and Sandy Row to the Malone Ridge, whence it was possible to travel to Lisburn, Hillsborough and beyond, or to swing eastwards across Shaw's Bridge into County Down. As the volume of traffic increased, a second southerly route, the Lisburn Road, was opened in 1819, described much later rather extravagantly as 'Belfast's great No. 1 main artery.'

The peak of the coaching era was reached in the 1840s and 1850s. By then Ireland was acquiring a railway network which, in the case of Ulster, converged on Belfast. The line that eventually formed the Great Northern Railway ran from Belfast down the Lagan valley and so to the rich pastoral counties of south and west Ulster, with a southerly link to Louth and Dublin. A second system comprised the Belfast and Northern Counties Railway. It originated in a line from Belfast to Ballymena and extended northwards to Ballymoney, Coleraine and Portrush. From Coleraine a line swung westwards, thus extending Belfast's hinterland into regions traditionally served by Londonderry. Finally, the Belfast and County Down Railway served the south-eastern corner of the province. As these networks were developed, linens and agricultural goods were moved with increasing ease to the port of Belfast. In return they carried cheap Manchester cottons, Birmingham hardware and Staffordshire pottery into Ulster's farmhouses and cottages, as well as cheap American grain and bacon, and Empire tea, sugar and groceries, items that gradually weaned the rural population away from its traditional diet of potatoes, oatmeal and dairy produce.

In the second half of the nineteenth century Belfast grew more rapidly than any other city in the British Isles. It was the last of the Industrial Revolution cities, its prosperity resting principally on the textile, engineering and shipbuilding trades. In 1901 these three industries employed almost one-third of the work force of 164,000. Belfast was one of the great linen producing centres of the world and

Joy's Paper Mill, c. 1840 (attributed to Hugh Frazer, Ulster Museum oil painting).

Joy's Paper Mill, c. 1882 (water colour by Ernest Hamford, Ulster Museum). The 1841 census recorded 21 paper makers in Belfast, working in Joy's paper mill located on the site of the old gas office in Ormeau Avenue. These two illustrations demonstrate the importance of water power in early Belfast industry. The river is the Blackstaff, looking rather more enchanting than it possibly was in reality.

certainly the greatest in the British Isles. In 1910, for example, 82 per cent of all linen spindles in the UK were located in Ireland, about one-third of them in Belfast and most of the rest elsewhere in Ulster. Weaving was even more concentrated in Belfast, which in 1910 contained 21,000 of the 58,000 powerlooms in the British Isles. Another 13,000 looms were located in other parts of Ulster; the other Irish counties could muster only 3,000 between them. Three-quarters of all Irish linen was sold abroad, the bulk of it to the USA. In this industry Belfast's hinterland stretched around the world.

Belfast dominance in shipbuilding was, arguably, even greater. In the years 1900–13, when the UK was the world's greatest shipbuilding nation, 17 per cent of total UK tonnage was built in Ireland, almost all of it by the two Belfast yards of Harland and Wolff and Workman and Clark. There were a few small shipbuilding and repairing yards in Dublin, Londonderry and elsewhere, but their importance was declining and their output negligible. Belfast's importance was, in fact, greater than simple percentages indicate, for her yards concentrated on big ships for the merchant marine and Royal Navy, not small tramp and coastal steamers. It was around the Belfast shipbuilding industry, and to a lesser extent the textile industry, that the engineering industry clustered. Except for steam-engine manufacture, agricultural machinery, railway engineering and cycle making, Belfast was dominant in all branches of engineering in Ireland, and its textile machinery, in particular, had world-wide renown.

It is thus easy to understand why Stephen Gwynn, a perceptive observer who wrote one of the earliest serious assessments of Irish towns in 1915, was so struck by the distinctiveness of Belfast. It was, he wrote 'one of the greatest manufacturing towns [and] also one of the greatest sea ports in the United Kingdom'. The characteristic sounds of Belfast, he continued, were those of industry. 'Hammer, hammer, hammer—that . . . is the noise we want to hear in Ireland; money, money, money, bread, bread, bread—stay at home and earn it—that was the tune it went to.' It was a tune almost unique to Belfast. The contrast with Dublin is striking. At the beginning of the nineteenth century, Dublin was the second city of the Empire with a population of over 180,000. By the mid-century its population had grown more or less in line with that of Ireland as a whole to 258,000. By 1891 the population of Dublin city had actually fallen to 245,000. Greater Dublin, indeed, had a population of 347,000, somewhat bigger than Belfast's population, but it was only by constantly redrawing the city's boundary that Dublin could—in the words of an MP—remain ahead of Belfast and keep its place 'in reality, as it is in

Malone House, 1832 (Joseph Malloy, Ulster Museum). With growing wealth and confidence, Belfast's leading businessmen built themselves substantial residences on the outskirts of the city. Artistic licence has created for Malone House an Alpine setting. Shaw's Bridge strides the Lagan like a Roman viaduct and Cave Hill towers like the Eiger.

name the first city of Ireland in all respects'. Unlike Belfast, Dublin's industries—milling, tanning, food processing, shoemaking, silk and woollens, furniture—were in decline, with the exception of brewing. It became essentially a shop-keeping and servicing city, devoid even of those administrative and governmental functions that contributed to its elegance and prosperity in the eighteenth century, overshadowed in wealth and rivalled in size by the upstart Belfast.

Belfast, of course, did not lose its older functions as a market town as its great industries developed. The streets were lined with furniture shops, hat emporiums, medical halls, insurance offices, photographic studios, and many other businesses which relied not only on the city's thronging thousands, but on the custom of a rural population that found Belfast increasingly accessible as railway and tramway networks expanded. Some businesses actively touted for country trade, such as the High Street photographer William Abernethy who provided all-purpose love letters to accompany his photographs, including an opening stanza clearly aimed at rustic clientele:

Dear Sarah Jane, you've often said
That, whun a went'tae see Belfast
A ocht tae get my picter taen,
So, dear, a've got it tuk at last.

And with the hale and hearty coming to Belfast to do their shopping or to have their photographs taken, so the ailing came looking for cures. As early as 1841 a 'confectioner and pastry baker' in Union Street, proclaimed to the Ulster public that he had a variety of confections for sale including 'Warm Stomach Rock', recommended 'for a sore throat or pain in the stomach. It expels wind, changes the

High Street c. 1910 (Welch Collection, Ulster Museum).

acrimony of the bile, strengthens the stomach and promotes digestion and the different secretions'. Those who wished their remedies to be more refined, and to come from more elevated practitioners than pastry cooks, obtained prescriptions from physicians and had them dispensed at Grattan's, Belfast's best-known

Castle Street 1910 (Welch Collection, Ulster Museum). Although industry expanded, the town remained an important shopping and commercial centre for the whole of Ulster. In these two photographs we see a medical hall, hat emporium, photographer's studio, florist's shop, insurance office, estate agent's office, furnishers, and hardware shop.

chemist. In the 1820s Grattan's business was scattered throughout Ulster. Thus in July 1825 they dispatched medicines worth 2/3d to a lady in Holywood; in October, quinine, liniments and other substances were sent to a doctor in Antrim, presumably for his practice; other orders, including a rather intimidating 'enema apparatus', were dispatched to Dromore, Lisburn, Carrick and elsewhere. The business expanded throughout the nineteenth century and into the next, and 'on one typical day in January 1910 Grattan's . . . made up prescriptions for Fivemiletown, Cookstown, Newtownbutler and Downpatrick.'

In these many ways Belfast exercised a powerful sway over the countryside. But its influence took other forms. As has been shown, nineteenth-century Belfast was the centre of a distinctive Ulster society. From its early days it had been a cradle of presbyterianism and by the mid-nineteenth century, as the outcome of the great theological battles between the two Henrys—Montgomery and Cooke—it had become the bastion of a conservative evangelical presbyterianism that permeated the whole of east Ulster. In the early 1800s the Academical Institution trained men for its ministry, but in 1853 the Presbyterian College was founded. This drew young men from throughout the province, whence they returned imbued with a staunch orthodox Calvinism.

The 1841 census had recorded 256 people in Belfast 'Ministering to Education'. By 1901 the number had grown to almost 2,000. The

The Royal Belfast Academical Institution 1902 (Hogg Collection, Ulster Museum). The photograph was taken before the College of Technology was built, but some building materials are already assembled.

schools ranged in size and ambition from private schools run by earnest ladies, to renowned institutions such as the Royal Belfast Academical Institution. These drew pupils from many parts of Ulster. In the late nineteenth century, for example, the daughters of the McKinney family at Carnmoney were sent to Miss Robinson's Educational Establishment for Young Ladies on the Antrim Road, while the sons went to Inst. These schools, for all the declared intention of Inst. to be 'perfectly unbiassed by religious distinctions', underpinned the values of the protestant English and Scottish settlers which had made Belfast and its region different from the rest of Ireland. To that extent, therefore, there is substance in the charge of Stephen Gwynn that the city destroyed the indigenous culture of Antrim and Down. Largely, but not quite. Inst. in 1819 offered classes in Irish 'to the antiquarian who would trace the origins of names and customs; the general philologist, and the person who expects to have intercourse with the West and South of Ireland'. Later, in 1852, Hugh McDonnell of Millfield described himself in the street directory as 'a teacher of Irish', and a little later, in 1860–1, Queen's College installed a 'Professor of Keltic Languages'.

Nineteenth-century Belfast, then, was a market town that became an industrial city. Throughout the metamorphosis the links between town and country remained strong. The town provided goods and services, employment and wealth, education and entertainment, for the people of Ulster, particularly for the inhabitants of the neighbouring counties of Antrim and Down. Yet, as has been shown, the connection was not all one way. Sybil Gribbon, writing of Edwardian Belfast, remarks that it was 'above all a port', and that 'the small mixed farms of Ulster were the backbone of Belfast's trade'.

Belfast Pork Market, c. 1910 (Hogg Collection, Ulster Museum). Pigs come to market. In the early 20th century Belfast was still a country town.

Without that produce—butter, bacon, oats and linen—Belfast would never have developed beyond its station as a muddy crossing point at the mouth of an undistinguished river. And as the products of Ulster's countryside went out through the port, so there came in return all those things that a flourishing populace demanded. Once Belfast's own industries developed, so they recruited labour from the countryside. The newcomers included episcopalians from south Ulster and catholics from the north and west, as well as country-born presbyterians. The arrival of large numbers of catholics was especially important. At the beginning of the nineteenth century catholics comprised less than one-tenth of the city's population, by 1861 one-third, and in 1901 one-quarter. With their coming the sectarian conflict that had been a feature of rural Ulster in the late eighteenth century became an urban phenomenon, and the city developed the areas of religious segregation that are familiar today. In this respect too, Belfast was of a piece with the Ulster countryside which had helped to create it.

12. The Edwardian city

Brenda Collins

The opening of Belfast's new City Hall in 1906 symbolised for many of its citizens their entitlement to civic pride born out of commercial success. For them, as for so many other British citizens, the Edwardian period appeared as the ever-rising crest of a wave of prosperity. Such confidence had a sound basis, for the thirty year period before the First World War was one when the commercial and economic life of Belfast enjoyed greater prosperity than ever before or since. The products of its staple industries were in demand by world markets and even though the rewards may not have been equally distributed, all but the poorest classes benefited. For skilled workers in particular, the economic achievements provided stability of employment and the chance of a steady and respectable style of living. In retrospect, however, the period has been aptly described as one between a verdict and a sentence. No matter how much Belfast was dependent on world markets for its existence, its character was determined by events which were internal to Ireland.

Belfast had grown from virtual obscurity at the beginning of the nineteenth century. Between 1835 and 1850 the population of the town had doubled to almost 90,000; between 1850 and 1901 it increased about fourfold to 350,000 people. By Edwardian times Belfast was not only the twelfth largest city in the United Kingdom, it was also bigger than Dublin, much to the latter's irritation. The geographical spread of the city reflected its roots in early industrialisation. At the very beginning of the nineteenth century Belfast had had a shortlived cotton industry. This had been located west of the city centre, around Smithfield, where streams provided the essential water power for spinning. Subsequently, many of these early cotton mills became linen mills and the foundations of Belfast's linen industry were laid. By 1900 the picture of densely packed industrial housing overshadowed by mill chimneys was characteristic of west Belfast though it was by no means confined to it.

The second of the dual prongs of the city's prosperity, shipbuilding, bestowed an equally unmistakable identity on the neighbourhood of Ballymacarret, 'over the bridge'. Iron shipbuilding had been put on a firm footing in 1853 with the takeover by Robert Hickson of a Queen's Island site, and his appointment of Edward Harland as manager the following year. The subsequent

Queen's Bridge. View from Oxford Street taken between 1906–1911 (Welch Collection, Ulster Museum). The sailing ship at the coal wharf seems almost from a different era.

story of Harland, who bought over the yard and went on to establish the firm of Harland and Wolff in 1861 is well known. The firm expanded tenfold and, with Pirrie now in effective control, employed about 9,000 by the beginning of the twentieth century, 12,000 by the outbreak of war. Workman and Clark, the other major yard, established in the 1880s, expanded at a similar rate, and in 1902 their output of 750,000 tons was the greatest of any single yard in Britain.

Changes in the municipal boundaries were slow to reflect the increase in population. As a result, the provision of civic amenities, such as road maintenance, sewage, parks and tramways, dependent on the income from rate-payers, was restricted by lack of cash. The most powerful force in the argument for extending the boundary was that the new suburbs of Strandtown, Ballyhackamore and Knock on the east, Malone on the south and Ballymurphy on the west should share the rate burden as they benefited from the amenities. In 1895 a sub-committee of the city council prepared a private Bill to extend the municipal boundary to the parliamentary limits. Fifteen wards were created out of the original five dating from 1853, a reflection of the extent to which reform was overdue. Two legacies remain from these boundary changes. The municipal area thus constituted remains until the present day, though even in the Edwardian period many of those who enjoyed Belfast's amenities by day travelled home each night beyond the city boundary. The second legacy was more important for the development of social relations within the community as a whole for the 1896 boundaries were constructed so as to reflect the segregated housing pattern of industrial Belfast. Two of the new fifteen wards, Falls and Smithfield, gained a perpetuating catholic majority. Thus, as Joe Devlin, the nationalist MP, predicted with foreboding, the guarantee of limited catholic representation in local politics institutionalised a sectarian pattern of voting for the years to come.

The political economy of Belfast on the eve of the First World War thus reflected an established pattern of housing. Its roots were in the early industrial development of the city and the subsequent exodus of the middle and professional classes from their Donegall Square townhouses, whose grandeur had declined as the smoky industrial chimneys increased, to the more spacious and airy suburbs. Doctors and financiers, solicitors and architects now separated their home lives from their professional lives. This movement was most obvious in the south of the city where the middle class suburbs of the Malone ridge and the University area were a much more healthy environment than lower down Dublin Road near the 'nuisance' of the River Blackstaff, which was contaminated by the refuse of mills and factories. Late nineteenth-century medical opinion might not have recognised the term 'atmospheric pollution' but the desirability of a south Belfast address stemmed as much from prosaic matters of health and illness as it did from notions of grandeur. The middle class took their institutions with them; the Academical Institution opened a preparatory school in Malone, Victoria College catered for the education of young ladies, while Fisherwick church moved from its central town position to a choice suburban site.

Carlisle Circus, c. 1906–1910 (Welch Collection, Ulster Museum). An important junction for trams and hackney carriages.

To the north of the city centre overlooking the shores of Belfast Lough, the former deerpark of the Donegalls was divided into

Oldpark and Newpark. Northwards from Carlisle Circus areas such as Mount Vernon, Parkmount and Duncairn and the loughside estates of the Grove, Fortwilliam and Skegoniel grew from the parcelling out of villa parkland into attractive sites for the aspiring lower middle class of commercial clerks and manufacturers' agents. An imaginative attempt to capture the interest of this growing section of Belfast society was made by Sir Robert McConnell, who promoted a Garden City near Cliftonville Circus, with houses selling at £240. Unfortunately, even the promise of pleasure gardens and a bandstand was not enough to win many converts among clerks earning £120 per year, and the scheme failed.

Across the Lagan, beyond industrial Ballymacarett and Lagan village, a vigorous suburban development was also under way, and the estates of Ormeau, Ravenhill, Rosetta, Annadale, Knock, Belmont and Stormont were gradually replaced by neat avenues and parades of new villas. Apart from the area around Strandtown and much of Ormeau and Rosetta, both of which were pre-1900, most of this suburban growth took place within the newly extended boundary of 1896. Their later construction meant that, in the main, the villas were more modest than those of south Belfast. Although some of the wealthiest and most powerful men in the city lived in the Belmont area, the chief demand for this housing, before 1914, came not from the professional elite of the city but from the shopkeepers and independent merchants whose businesses had benefited from the general increase in spending power.

Queen's Quay Station, Belfast and County Down Railway (Welch Collection, Ulster Museum). Taken after the re-opening of the rebuilt station in 1912, this was probably the occasion of a special excursion.

In the city centre, private residences were replaced by commercial premises. The five department stores of Arnott's, Robb's, the Bank Buildings, Anderson and McAuley, and Robinson and Cleaver (not to mention Brand and Co., ladies tailors) were testimony to the vitality of commerce. Sawers in High Street catered for the high class end of the fish and butchery trade, while S. D. Bell's in Ann Street did the same for groceries. For the more modest spenders there were four branches of Lipton's and six of the Home and Colonial Stores while the Belfast Co-operative Society had eight branches and a membership, in 1905, of 2,500. In another sphere of consumer spending, footwear, English-based multiple stores had been established; Tyler's had eight city centre branches and Manfield's had two.

Transport to and from the suburbs was provided by the Belfast Street Tramways Company, established in the 1870s, and taken over by the corporation in 1904. A twopenny fare was the maximum, regardless of distance, and cheap workman's tickets were also issued at certain hours in the morning and evening. In 1897 the Company kept over one thousand horses and employed a large workforce to look after their stabling, in addition to the employees who drove the trams. But the days of the ten and eleven year old trace boys and their horses were shortlived, for the corporation introduced electrification, when it bought the Company, at a total cost of nearly £1 million.

The vast majority of Belfast's working people, however, made use of trams only on high days and holidays. Indeed tram fares were considered luxuries by the Board of Guardians when it was calculating the amount of poor relief to give a family. Most people lived within walking distance of their places of work, often in houses which had been built to the dismally low standards of the mid-nineteenth century. The oldest houses were in and around Smithfield, site of the early linen mills. Courts and entries dating from this period were only beginning to be cleared by demolition in the 1890s and early 1900s, and even with municipal help only 1,200 houses, containing just under 7,000 people, were affected. Mid-nineteenth-century housing was regulated only to the extent that a nine foot square back yard was required and the yards were set back to back with no passageway between. Although rear access was mandatory in all houses built after 1878, general progress was slow; in 1898 it was estimated that 20,000 of the 70,000 houses in the city still had no back access, and so all their refuse, including the contents of the ashpit privies, had to be carried through the living accommodation to the street for collection by the corporation scavengers. Still, the legislation on improved minimum standards of housing was in force during the period of Belfast's building boom. About 50,000 houses were built in the last twenty years of the century, with a peak of nearly 4,500 in 1898, followed by a slump, to one-sixth of that level, which persisted through the Edwardian period. The overdevelopment was essentially one of speculative building of three-bedroomed, terrace houses for the middle income sector of the market.

Castle Place looking towards the Bank Buildings, c. 1906–1910 (Welch Collection, Ulster Museum). Robb's is on the right.

The typical new houses for the working men of the Edwardian period were the 'kitchen' and 'parlour' houses. Though in construction there was little difference between them, because both occupied a similar street frontage and had four rooms and a small scullery, the differences in accommodation and social status were real enough to the families who lived in them. The parlour house had a sitting room or parlour on the ground floor with a kitchen and scullery behind it, and two bedrooms on the upper floor. The front door opened onto a small hall containing the stairs and doors to the parlour and kitchen. The parlour was generally reserved for use on Sundays or for visitors. In contrast, the kitchen houses had no separate sitting room, but a kitchen on the ground floor at the front, with a bedroom and scullery at the rear. The stairs led from the kitchen to a landing with doors opening to the two bedrooms. The weekly rent of kitchen houses was about 3/6 to 4/- while the rent of the parlour house was 4/6 to 5/-. Kitchen houses were more popular not merely because they were cheaper but because they offered more sleeping accommodation. Generally the front bedroom was much bigger than the back so it was often used by the parents and all the girls, with sons sleeping in the back bedroom. The downstairs rooms were no more than fourteen feet square. Older houses usually had three rooms rather than four, a kitchen/scullery on the ground floor and two bedrooms upstairs. Their rents were lower, reflecting the inferior accommodation, at 2/6 to 3/6d per week. Five-roomed houses, which had a third bedroom built in the return over the scullery were occupied by those with skilled trades; only they could afford the greater outlay of 5/- to 6/3d per week and had the relative job security to consider such an expenditure worthwhile.

Though the type of house people chose to live in was of course dependent on their earnings, for many the religion of their

Upper North Street, junction with Carrick Hill, 1894 (Welch Collection, Ulster Museum). Taken shortly before the slum clearance of Carrick Hill, this photograph conveys dampness and dreariness. Note the pawnbroker's sign on the left.

neighbours was as important. During the second half of the nineteenth century the proportion of catholics in the population of Belfast declined from over one-third in 1861 to less than one-quarter by 1901. The city developed not only a protestant but a presbyterian identity, as religious affiliation became increasingly a badge of social identification. The influx of rural Ulstermen and women in the 1870s and 1880s was primarily a protestant influx, from Antrim, Down and Armagh, and there were few migrants from other southern counties to redress the balance. Of the rural-born catholics who did move to the city there were considerably more women than men, particularly among the young people—women, of course, were able to find ready employment in the linen industry and in domestic service. It seems that catholic men from rural Ulster looked more to emigration than the big city of Belfast as a means of getting on in life. This attitude was scarcely surprising in view of the repeated demonstrations of anti-catholic feeling at intervals during the nineteenth century, which often resulted in rioting. The Belfast commissioners' report on the riots in 1886 illustrated how the civil disorders led to the creation of separate protestant and catholic neighbourhoods:

> The extremity to which party and religious feeling has grown in Belfast is shown strikingly by the fact that the people of the artisan and labouring classes . . . dwell to a large extent in separate quarters, each of which is given up almost entirely to persons of one particular faith, and the boundaries of which are sharply defined. In the district of West Belfast, the great thoroughfare of the Shankill Road with the network of streets running into it . . . is an almost entirely protestant district . . . the great catholic quarter is due south of the Shankill district and consists of the thoroughfare known as the Falls Road and the streets running south of it. Due south of the Falls district is Grosvenor Street, almost entirely inhabited by protestants so that the catholic quarter lies between two protestant districts..

In this catholic quarter, so clearly demarcated, many of the streets were, by 1901, virtually 100 per cent catholic. But what was more important for the development of neighbourhood identity within these streets, as opposed to civic pride as a whole, was that 45 per cent of all the catholic families in Belfast lived here. As the oldest developed area of the city, it was the one with the poorest housing. Thus not only were catholic families more likely than protestants to live in poorer housing with fewer rooms, they also had fewer amenities. According to the city valuation of 1901 only 50 per cent of catholic households, in comparison with 70 per cent of protestant households, had a gas supply to their houses. Within a few years the corporation, eternally alert to new sources of revenue, provided every house with free gas fittings in the form of a meter, one light bracket and one gas ring to sit on the hob of the fire. A fixed bath,

Beatty's Entry off Hamill Street, 1910 (Hogg Collection, Ulster Museum). Some of the oldest and poorest houses in the city yet the boys appear well enough dressed against the cold weather.

however, was a luxury beyond all but the top level of working class society, and in this respect also catholic families were worse off—only one in sixteen catholic families had a fixed bath in their houses compared with one in six protestant families. The sharing of common hardship, if not downright poverty, reinforced neighbourliness. If unemployment or sickness struck, families moved in with one another or lent practical help. The local pawnshop was another recourse in case of short-term need. Regular pawning of a suit on a Monday to be redeemed on the Saturday was a mark of prudent budgeting rather than a sign of fecklessness. Self-help on a neighbourhood scale was how such communities survived, and children's earnings were often crucial to the family budget. Belfast's Board of Guardians granted the lowest amount of outdoor relief (both in terms of recipients and amounts) in the British Isles. The Liberal welfare reforms of 1906–1914, however, were the beginning of state intervention on the grounds of need. The most immediate aid came from the introduction in 1909 of a 5/- old age pension. This was given to those over seventy who had an income of less than 10/- a week, and was said to have so much increased filial affection in Ireland that 'if an old age pensioner begins to cough, so much anxiety is displayed by his family that the doctor is dragged out of his home . . . to prolong the life of this eligible member of the family'.

Castle Junction 1905 (Hogg Collection, Ulster Museum). A view still easily recognisable today even without the horse-drawn trams.

If Westminster's social reforms for the aged and the sick bridged the religious divide, they did not alter the job structure of those of working age. The main industries, shipbuilding and linen, certainly provided employment for all, though the labour force in engineering,

Cornmarket; premises of S. Stokesberry, quality butcher, and John McAfee and Son, high class boot maker, 1913 (Welch Collection, Ulster Museum). McAfee's claimed on their window pane to supply the Duke of York (later George V).

iron manufacture and shipbuilding was only 14 per cent catholic. Even in the linen industry catholics were under-represented, at only 21 per cent of the male workforce. Moreover, elements of status were involved which made the catholic man's position worse than the bare job categories imply. The shipyard workers and those in the Sirocco Works, Mackie Bros., and Coombe Barbour, who were regarded as Belfast's 'aristocracy of labour', earned about £2 per week on the eve of the First World War (and much more during the War itself). Their skilled jobs were closed except to those youngsters taken on at thirteen years of age to serve a seven year apprenticeship. Informal networks of family and friends thus reinforced the hold which the protestant community had obtained over the engineering trades at the time of their expansion in the 1870s and 1880s. This was given further backing from the craft unionisation which developed through the Belfast and District United Trades' Council. Highly paid jobs in the linen industry too, such as those of foremen and spinning masters, were more often held by protestant men, particularly those who had started work in the mills at thirteen or fourteen years of age. At the lower end of the social scale, catholics made up nearly one-third of the general labourers, according to the 1901 census, though they were only 24 per cent of the population as a whole. Labourers suffered most from low wage levels, longest working hours and insecure employment dependent on the seasons or a change in trading fortunes. Their weekly wages were around 16/- to 19/-, in many cases less than half those of the tradesmen they worked to. Often strikes or short time working reduced this considerably. At the docks, for example, where of the 1,500 men employed in 1911, 40 per cent were catholic, casual workers were employed by the day to discharge general goods, grain, timber and coal, as they came in.

They were paid 5/- for a ten hour day with perhaps no more than four days work in a week. Even labourers engaged permanently as coal fillers, discharging coal cargoes, earned only 22/- to 24/- per week.

The domination of shipbuilding, engineering and linen has tended to obscure the wide variety of the city's industrial activities. Printing, lithography and bookbinding employed about 1,400 men at the turn of the century. The Belfast Ropeworks Company had been founded in 1873; by 1900 it was the largest in the world, covering a site of forty acres at Connswater, under its managing director W. H. Smiles, son of Samuel Smiles, Victorian advocate of self-help. Whiskey was distilled and blended by Dunville's, Mitchell's, Peter Keegan and Co., and a score of lesser businesses. Mineral waters were another celebrated Belfast export. These reputedly originated in the pure water of the Cromac springs, which were first transformed into aerated drinking water by Grattan's the chemists before the mid-nineteenth century. Fifty years later the substantial soft drinks industry was led by Corry's, Ross's, Lyle and Kinahan and Cantrell and Cochrane. Their products were particularly popular in India, Africa and South America, where colonial administrators welcomed the refreshing club ale and club kola, not to mention 'sparkling Montserrat, the drink for the gouty and rheumatic', lithia water, piperazine water, cinneverto and 'ginger ale for Export (extra strong)'. Last in the range of consumer items, and catering more for home tastes were the two tobacco firms of Gallaher's and Murray's, and the sweet manufacturer W. J. Shaw and Sons. The latter was an example of a large firm rising out of small beginnings, for W. J. Shaw's business grew out of his wife's corner shop in Sandy Row,

A fire at Marsh's biscuit factory, Donegall Street, 1905 (Hogg Collection, Ulster Museum) The horse-drawn carriage of the fire brigade can be seen in the background. The little boy in the foreground is typically attired, bare-footed but wearing a cap.

from which he travelled daily selling her stock of goods in outlying areas. His move from retailing to the manufacture of boiled sweets and clove rock was based on his personal experience of the newly-existing market for bought 'sweeties' among the young and fancy-free with money in their pockets. Shaw's success was typical of that of the Edwardian entrepreneur.

View of new City Hall and dust-cart (sic) 1904 (Hogg Collection, Ulster Museum). David Allen and Sons of Belfast claimed to be the 'largest billposting firm in the world'. Hoardings were the picture gallery of the poor man.

The overwhelming dominance of the linen industry, however, was the reason why, in sharp contrast to the rest of Ireland, nearly two-fifths of the city's total labour force was female. Almost 23,000 women worked in some branch of the linen trade, and another 5,500 in the making up trades. Altogether they made up 70 per cent of the industry's workforce. In contrast only about 6,500 women were in domestic service, reflecting the greater freedom and higher wages of mill work. Though the domination of women in clerical jobs was still in the future there were about 2,500 female commercial clerks and 'typewriters' in 1911. Nurses and schoolteachers accounted for another 2,000 women. As with their menfolk, catholic women were more likely to be found in the less attractive occupations. Within the linen industry they were working in the mills rather than the weaving factories, while over two-fifths of the domestic servants in 1911 were catholic, but only one-seventh of the clerks.

For women, the most sought-after jobs in the linen industry were in the embroidery and making-up trades, working in sewing warehouses or at home. Finishing aprons and handkerchiefs or embroidering collars and cuffs was considered to carry higher prestige than either spinning or weaving. It was cleaner and airier than mill or factory work, so girls going to and from the workroom did not carry the stamp of their working environment in the form of the smell of engine fumes or discoloured clothing. Work using the Singer sewing machine, in what had come to be known as Irish embroidery, was a 'sweated trade' for the many wives whose husbands were in casual or low-paid work. Payment of about 9d–11d per dozen (about 1½d per hour) was made for the embroidery of handkerchiefs, which were then put on sale for 6/- or more per dozen. Yet homework, despite its low rates, was a favoured employment, because it could be combined with household duties and it enabled the wives of status-conscious skilled tradesmen to add to the family income without publicly undermining the idea of the husband as provider.

As a city devoted to money making, Belfast had millionaires but no resident leisured class. Lord Shaftesbury's household, with its nineteen domestic servants recorded in the census of 1901, was at the head of society. Men such as Pirrie, and others whose industrial and commercial acumen had brought them wealth, were more likely to indulge in conspicuous consumption outside Belfast. One exception, which demonstrated that the wealth was there, was Pirrie's decision to host a banquet in honour of Lord Dufferin in 1896, when a specially-chartered boat sailed from London to Belfast for the occasion, equipped with all the cutlery, linens and the staff of

Children at the back entrance of North Thomas Street National School. 1912 (Hogg Collection, Ulster Museum).

a leading catering firm. At a more modest level of the employing class, entertainment was synonymous with family outings. The family of David Allen, printer and billposter, was accustomed to set off after church on Sundays for a sail on Belfast Lough, 'loaded with picnic baskets from which liberal provision of stout and whisky had not been omitted'.

Elementary education was neither compulsory nor universal at the turn of the century. Paradoxically, in many ways the children who came from the poorest families were the best catered for. They were the ones who were 'half timers' in the mills, and in 1907 there were over 3,800 children under thirteen working half-time in the Belfast mills for about 3/6d per week. They worked a half-time system of alternate days in the mill and at school. Millowners were held responsible for ensuring their 'half timers' attended school and often they established their own schools on the premises. Because there was not yet compulsory school attendance, the education received during half-time employment was, for some Edwardian children, the most sustained and continuous period of learning they received. The rest were dependent on church schools, or, if they could pay the fees, the private institutions. The churches, particularly the Church of Ireland, were unable to cope with the increasing numbers requiring schooling, and presbyterian councillors saw no need to make good the deficiencies of the wealthier church by demanding an educational levy on the rates. In 1911 there were 276 National Schools in the city with an enrolment which amounted to only 70 per cent of children aged 5 to 15. Even counting privately

A laboratory attendant in the Dairy Department of Belfast Co-operative Society's depot, Ravenhill Avenue, c. 1913 (Hogg Collection, Ulster Museum). A far cry from milk sold in open cans.

owned schools, over 15,000 children were without school places. For those at school the annual inspectors' reports complained consistently of gross overcrowding—401 children in a school in Ballymacarrett with proper accommodation for only 209. On the eve of the First World War it was acknowledged that Belfast (as well as Dublin) was twenty years behind many English authorities in its educational provisions.

In general, however, standards of living in Edwardian Belfast were no worse than in comparable English cities. Certainly infant death rates were higher than in the Ulster countryside, about 150 infants in every 1,000 died at birth or within the first three months of life, but these rates were exceeded in Leeds, Liverpool, Manchester, Birmingham and Dublin. Not until the link between contaminated food and gastro-intestinal infections had been understood would babies survive in greater numbers. Belfast's dairymen, however, were to continue selling their milk from open cans on carts until the 1920s; though the Co-op established a reputation for quality and hygiene. Infectious diseases such as whooping cough, measles and scarlet fever were the main killers of children. The persistence of typhoid, which accounted for 219 deaths in 1896, was evidence of an inadequate water supply, and it was said in 1906 that the extent of endemic typhoid was such that 'no other city or town of the United Kingdom equals or even approaches it in this respect'. Conditions improved greatly with the appointment of a medical officer of health who began to enforce controls on the discharge of sewage into Belfast Lough, as well as byelaws on the sale of shellfish from street barrows. Consumption continued to be the major killer of adults, accounting for nearly one in every six notified deaths in the city. The 65,536 cards entitled 'Information for Consumptive People and those living with them', which were distributed in Belfast's mills and factories in 1908, are a chilling reminder of the inevitability with which the disease was regarded.

In one respect at least, variety in diet, the Belfast working man fared better than his country cousins. Many observers were quick to castigate wives who failed to rear their families on wheaten bread, buttermilk, potatoes and broth, and turned instead to pan bread, margarine, tea, sugar and condensed milk—yet who could blame them if they had no ovens in which to bake bread, if the buttermilk and butter sold in the streets was covered with flies, and if broth required too long to simmer for women working a fifty-five hour week in the mills? The basics of the Ulster diet were being replaced by a variety of shop-bought food imported from throughout the Empire and beyond—New Zealand mutton chops at 9d per lb, American cheddar cheese at 8d per lb, Danish butter, cheaper than Irish at 1/2d per lb. The success of the Italian icecream saloons run by the Macaris and Fuscos in Peter's Hill and Great Victoria Street demonstrated that there was money to be spent beyond the bare necessities of life. They provided an alternative to the traditional

Bakers Exhibition award, 1907 (Hogg Collection, Ulster Museum). Quality control and socialist principles were a formidable combination.

outlet for hard-earned leisure, the public house. Changing attitudes to heavy spirit drinking, coupled with Lloyd George's 1908 budget duty of 8/- per gallon on spirits, did as much as the Irish Temperance League to encourage respectability among the working class.

On the eve of the First World War Belfast had a reputation for hard work and hard leisure, vigorous commercialism often at the expense of subtlety and refinement. Louis MacNeice summarised the view:

> See Belfast, devout and profane and hard,
> Built on reclaimed mud, hammers playing in the shipyard;
> Time punched with holes like a steel sheet, time
> hardening the faces, veneering with a grey and speckled rime
> The faces under the shawls and caps:

This image became increasingly appropriate as the Ulster unionists again began to organise opposition to home rule. Local affairs were overshadowed by the national question. By the end of 1913 the Ulster Volunteer Force had over 22,000 members in the city. In March 1914 a Belfast branch of the Irish Volunteers was formed and within six months it had over 3,000 men. Then world events in turn imposed their pattern on the local scene. In 1915 14,000 recruits from Belfast enlisted for king and country; 4,000 were believed to be catholics and 10,000 protestants. The outbreak of hostilities changed altogether the parameters on which Belfast's commercial pre-eminence rested. After the war, the Troubles ensuing from the creation of the Northern Ireland state wrecked the feeling of stability which characterised the Edwardian period.

Further reading

1. **Belfast to the end of the eighteenth century**

Benn, George *A history of Belfast From the earliest times to the close of the eighteenth century* Belfast, 1877.

Joy, Henry, and Bruce, William *Belfast Politics; or, A collection of the debates, resolutions and other proceedings of that town, 1792–3* Belfast, 1794.

Young, R. M. *Historical notices of old Belfast and its vicinity* Belfast, 1896; *The Town Book of the corporation of Belfast* Belfast, 1892.

2. **Lords and landlords: the Donegall family**

Maguire, W. A. 'The 1822 settlement of the Donegall estates', *Irish Economic and Social History* vol. 3, 1976.

'Lord Donegall and the sale of Belfast', *Economic History Review* second series, vol. 29, 1976.

'Ormeau House', *Ulster Journal of Archaeology* vol. 42, 1979.

3. **'Linenopolis': the rise of the textile industry**

Boyle, E. 'The Economic Development of the Irish Linen Industry, 1825–1913', unpublished Ph.D. thesis, Q.U.B. 1979.

Geary, F. 'The Rise and Fall of the Belfast Cotton Industry: Some Problems', *Irish Economic and Social History* 7, 1981.

Green, E. R. R. *The Lagan Valley* London, 1949.

Monaghan, J. J. 'The Rise and Fall of the Belfast Cotton Industry', *Irish Historical Studies* 3, 1942.

4. **The development of the port**

Belfast Harbour Commissioners *Centenary Volume 1847–1947* Belfast, 1947.

The port of Belfast: a review 1947–62 Belfast, 1962.

Harland, E. J. *Shipbuilding in Belfast* Belfast, 1884.

Owen, D. J. *A short history of the port of Belfast* Belfast, 1917.

5. **'The Northern Athens' and after**

Brown, Terence *Northern Voices: Poets in Ulster* Dublin, 1975.

Bell, Sam Hanna *The Theatre in Ulster* Dublin, 1972.

Cousins, James, and Cousins, Maynard E. *We Two Together* Madras, 1950.

O'Donoghue, D. J. *The Poets of Ireland* Dublin and London, 1912.

Ferguson, Lady M. C. *Sir Samuel Ferguson in the Ireland of his day* 2 vols, London, 1896.

6. **Of art and artists**

Anglesea, Martyn *The Royal Ulster Academy of Arts* Belfast, 1981.

Crookshank, Anne, and the Knight of Glin *The Painters of Ireland* London, 1978.

Gray, William *Science and Art in Belfast* Belfast, 1904.
Hewitt, John, and Snoddy, Theo *Art in Ulster: 1* Belfast, 1977.
Strickland, W. G. *A Dictionary of Irish Artists* Dublin and London, 1913.
Wilson, Judith C. *Conor 1881–1968* Belfast, 1981.

7. **Popular entertainment**
(Sources and Further reading)
Bell, Sam Hanna *The Theatre in Ulster* Dublin, 1972.
Lawrence, W. J. 'The Annals of the Old Belfast Stage' unpublished manuscript in the Linenhall Library, Belfast.

8. **Religion and secular thought 1800-75**
Allen, Robert *The Presbyterian College Belfast 1853–1953* Belfast, 1954.
Beckett, J. C., and Moody, T. W. *Queen's, Belfast 1845–1949 The historyof a university* Belfast, 1959.
Eve, A. S., and Creasey, C. H. *The life and work of John Tyndall* London, 1945.
Holmes, R. Finlay, *Henry Cooke* Belfast, 1981.

9. **Community relations and the religious geography 1800-86**
Crolly, George *The Life of the Most Rev. Doctor Crolly* Dublin, 1851.
Norman, E. R. *The Catholic Church and Ireland in the Age of Rebellion 1859–1873* London, 1965.
O'Hanlon, W. M. *Walks among the Poor of Belfast* Belfast, 1853.
Rogers, Patrick *St Peters Pro-Cathedral, Belfast 1866–1966* Belfast, 1967.

10. **Politics and the rise of the skilled working man**
Gibbon, Peter *The Origins of Ulster Unionism* Manchester, 1975.
Patterson, Henry *Class Conflict and Sectarianism* Belfast, 1980.

11. **The city and the country**
Green, E. R. R. 'Economic History', *Belfast in its Regional Setting: A Scientific Survey* in British Association For the Advancement of Science, Belfast, 1952.
Gribbon, Sybil 'An Irish City: Belfast 1911', in Harkness, David, and O'Dowd, Mary *The Town in Ireland* Belfast, 1981.
Gwynn, Stephen *The Famous Cities of Ireland* Dublin and London, 1915.
O'Byrne, Cathal *As I Roved Out* Belfast, 1946.

12. **The Edwardian era**
Gribbon, Sybil *Edwardian Belfast: A Social Profile* Belfast, 1982.
Hepburn, A. C., and Collins, B. 'Industrial Society: the Structure of Belfast 1901' in Roebuck, Peter (ed) *Plantation to Partition* Belfast, 1981.

General

Beckett, J. C. and Glasscock, R. E. *Belfast: the origin and growth of an industrial city* B.B.C., 1967

Hayward, Richard *Belfast through the ages* London, 1960
Jones, Emrys *A social geography of Belfast* London, 1960
Lowry, Mary *The story of Belfast and its surroundings* London, 1913
McConnell, J. *Presbyterianism in Belfast* Belfast, 1912
McNeice, J. F. *The Church of Ireland in Belfast* Belfast, 1931
Millin, S. Shannon *Sidelights on Belfast history* Belfast and London, 1932; *Additional sidelights on Belfast history* Belfast and London, 1932
Owen, D. J. *History of Belfast* Belfast, 1921
Pilson, J. A., *History of the rise and progress of Belfast* Belfast, 1846

Index

West
COLLEGE
South
North
College Square
Falls Road
Distillery
Sunday School
Browns Square
Glass Works
Millfield
King Street
Baptist Meet.
House of Correction
Place
Street
Queen Street
SMITHFIELD
Marquis Street
Wine Tavern
Wellington
Water
Fountain Street
West
Bishop Street
ROAD
Bridge
WHITE LINEN HALL
Square
Donegall Place
Hercules Street
Linen Hall Street
South
Donegall
Course
Fountain
RIVER BLACKSTAFF
Callander Street
East
Castle Street
Corn Market
Stephen's Street
2nd Seceding Meeting Ho.
Arthur Street
Alfred Street
Street
Paper Mill
William Street
George's Lane
Montgomery Street
Chichester
Street
POULTRY SQUARE
Henrietta
Bridge Cromack Street
Great Edward Street
May's Bridge
KINGS STORES
MAYS MARKET
MAY'S DOCK
HIGH STREET
STREET
ANN
Church Lane
Forest Lane
Prince's Street
Custom House Quay
Chichester Quay
Merchants Quay
Dock
Limekiln
Brown Linen Hall
DONEGALL
NORTH
WARING STREET
Bridge Street
Rosemary
Berry Street
Millers Lane
Hudsons Entry
May
May's Bridge
LONG BRIDGE
Arched 840 feet
PROPOSED SCITE OF NEW BRIDGE
1314 feet
SALT WORKS
WORKS
Vitriol Works
RIVER
LAGAN